10⁰⁰

Crafts and Craft Shows

Crafts and Craft Shows

HOW TO MAKE MONEY

PHIL KADUBEC

ALLWORTH PRESS
NEW YORK

08 07 06 05 04 03   8 7 6 5 4 3

Published by Allworth Press
An imprint of Allworth Communications
10 East 23rd Street, New York, NY 10010

Cover design by Douglas Design Associates, New York, NY

Page composition/typography by SR Desktop Services, Ridge, NY

Library of Congress Cataloging-in-Publication Data
Kadubec, Phil.
    Crafts and craft shows : how to make money / by Phil Kadubec.
        p.   cm.
    Includes index.
    ISBN 1-58115-060-1
    1. Handicraft—Marketing.   2. Craft festivals—Planning.   I. Title.
HD9999.H362 K33   2000
745.5'068'8—dc21   00-032782

Printed in Canada

"*The manufacturer who waits in the woods for the world to beat a path to his door is a great optimist. But the manufacturer who shows his 'mousetraps' to the world keeps the smoke coming out of his chimney.*"

—O. B. WINTERS

Dedication

To my wife Judy, with all my love and deep appreciation. Without her, there would be no book, because there would have been no crafts business. It was her inspiration and creativity that first sent us on our crafting journey. Her dedication, perseverance, never-give-up attitude, and optimistic spirit were what kept me going, and her ability to relate to people was what made our business a success. I just built the baskets, wrote the book, and was part of the odyssey on which she took us.

My everlasting thanks also to our son Mark, who stained thousands of baskets, enjoyed the journey during his young years, and so stoically endured it all as he grew to maturity. You kept me on schedule, son, and kept me laughing. As we stood side by side through all your young years, it was a joy to watch you grow up.

Contents

What You Are Not
The Need to Develop Self-Reliance
Naming Your Business
Your Personal Appearance
Your Business Card
The Most Trivial Things Can Be Important
Your Craft Show Schedule
The Importance of a Large Inventory to Your Sales
The Reality of the Craft Marketplace
Never Be Self-Satisfied
Try to Produce Something Different
Try to Stand Out from the Competition
Variety Is the Spice of Life
The Copycat
Know Yourself, Your Assets, and Your Limitations
Reevaluate the Crafts Business
Set Your Standard High
Keep Up with the Trends, Fads, and Even Eccentricities of Your Public
Continue Evaluating Yourself

The Difficulty of Pricing Your Craft
A Variety of Factors Affect Your Price
The Loss Leader
You Can't Make Constant Price Adjustments
The Hourly Wage Issue
Customer Reaction Can Help Determine Your Price
The Numbers Game of Pricing

Test Pricing
Once Again Variety
Adjust Your Inventory
The Special Order
Another Reason to Review Your Pricing Structure
Cash Flow

Get Professional Help
Open a Business Banking Account
Avoid Commingling Funds
Small Business Regulations, Resale Permits, and Licenses
Assessing Sales Tax to the Customer
The Resale Permit
Your Suppliers and Your Accounts
Catalogue Suppliers
Keeping Your Records
Business-Related Use of Your Vehicle
Establish a Mailing List
Buy a Cash Register
Design Patents, Copyright, and Trademarks
A Crucial Related Problem
Small Business Insurance
Merchant Charge Accounts
Accepting Checks
Your Business Work Routine
The Need for Record Keeping

How *Not* to Pick Your Shows
A Great Show Is a Relative Matter
Then There Is the Liar
More Conventional Means of Selecting Your Shows
Negatives about the Unsolicited or Personal Invitation
The Exception to the Rule
The Best Method of Selecting Your Shows
The Guide Book
Many Factors Will Influence Your Show Selection
Show Fees
Another Reality Check
Some General Advice

Appeal to the Customer's Senses and Sense of Self-Importance
Men at a Craft Show
Controlling Your Own Feelings

Wholesaling Your Product
Renting Floor Space in a Shop
Selling on Consignment
The Rep or Middle Man
More Unusual Methods of Selling Your Craft
The Television Market
The Internet
The End of the Craft Road or Taking a New Direction?
What Might Have Been
Rosie's Business Adventures and Misadventures
When to Retire and Preparing for It

Acknowledgments

URING THE SEVENTEEN YEARS THAT JUDY AND I participated in the craft world, numerous craftspeople assisted us in ways too varied to enumerate. Often we were ships in the night, passing by, never to meet again. To those people who may remember The Three Basketeers, and now read this book, our heartfelt thanks.

As I wrote this book, there were areas of the crafts business in which my knowledge was quite limited. It was therefore necessary to draw on the expertise of people who possessed that experience. I am deeply indebted to Wanda McAleese, group manager of Harvest Festival; Rhonda Blakely, promoter of Country Folk Art; Beth Weber, promoter for North Tahoe Fine Art Association; Rich Burleigh, promoter of Fire on the Mountain, and Rosie Lamar, for sacrificing their valuable time to answer my many questions, so that I might accurately represent the promotional and manufacturing side of the crafts business.

Throughout the years, some very special people provided advice and counsel, without which we would not have been successful. Our special thanks to Bill Campbell (Rocking Horse Bill), who was next to us in Arnold, California, on July 4, 1982, our first two-day craft show. What you taught us in two days, Bill, would have taken two years to learn.

To a most special couple, Jim and Fran Seeley, known in the business as Lord Jim, we extend our deepest appreciation for the friendship, help, and advice you extended throughout our career. Thanks to you, we moved into the "Big Time" arenas where the real money is to be made. We regret that our friendship must now be conducted across the so many miles that separate us. We miss and will always cherish the jokes, the laughs, the fun, the debates, and the work we enjoyed together. May your much deserved retirement in Maine fulfill your dreams.

Introduction

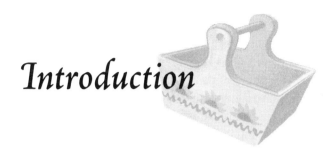

*D*URING THE THRIVING ECONOMIC CONDITIONS OF THE past two decades, an increasing number of individuals have ventured into creative, entrepreneurial businesses. Nowhere is that more evident than in the world of crafts. Everywhere you look, there is evidence of modern renderings of yesterday's treasures. Makers of furniture, wall coverings, home design, clothing, bedding, even cooking utensils, seek to reflect and imitate in their products the timeless love and attention to detail that the craftsmen of long ago put into their work.

This book is the product of our experience in the craft world. During the seventeen years that we devoted to it, Judy and I traveled the length and breadth of California and Nevada selling our creations in as many as thirty-five craft shows a year.

As it so often happens in the crafts business, our eventual product line and successful business began as a hobby. It then developed into a means to supplement my retirement income and quickly developed into a thriving, full-time occupation. We were known as The Three Basketeers.

There are thousands of such craft names throughout America today. The names represent the many people who design a unique product and assert their desire to be independent of systems, bureaucracies, and corporations by venturing out on the road to sell it. Throughout the years, we met doctors, lawyers, carpenters, engineers, teachers, plumbers—members of almost every profession and vocation. All had walked away from their planned and established careers to express a new-found talent and independence.

As we are being moved daily, sometimes kicking and screaming, into this new, highly technological society—sometimes referred to as a *disposable society*—the public's resistance to it may explain the endurance of the craft show and its thousands of exhibitors. More profound explanations we leave to social scientists.

We can only say that at every craft show, as our customers searched nostalgically for prized examples of a simpler period in our lives and in our history, we sensed them seeking durability and craving yesteryear. The crafts business may well be one of the last true vestiges of our nation's Free Enterprise System, alive and well every weekend across our land. Craftspeople probably influence the current trends in every marketplace far more than is recognized by the public or than craftsmen themselves may realize.

Maybe you are already one of these people. Or, perhaps you are just now considering entering the crafts business. If you are, whether you expect to do only a few shows a year, are already a veteran craftsman, or are newly entering the business on a full-time basis, we believe this book will assist you in your quest for financial success.

Of course, no book can help those who take a negative view of themselves or their product. We cannot help people who find excuses for their failure (and craftspeople have dozens) or those who waste time and energy complaining about how they are not appreciated. Nor is this a book for those who enjoy a nice hobby and then make a few gifts for family members and select friends at Christmastime. And this book definitely cannot help those who believe in creating "art for art's sake."

This book is directed to those individuals who, at craft shows week after week, put their talent on the line without sufficient financial reward. It is also dedicated to those who have yet to do their first show, but, believing in their product, are ready to test it in the marketplace and expect to earn a good living by doing so. Both must have faith in their creative abilities and must not be afraid of hard work—the two essential ingredients necessary to earn a substantial living. For, like every business endeavor, the crafts business is about making money, and there is plenty to be made. But, to make it, you must also be prepared to deal with reality.

Through the years, Judy and I met many people who possess a romantic, enchanted vision of the crafts business. Truthfully, that never-never land doesn't exist. To make a success of the business, that vision must be tempered with practicality and good judgment. There is nothing fascinating, enjoyable, or romantic about setting up your booth in some desolate parking lot or community park at five in the morning. Nor is there anything pleasurable about lugging your wares up and down the stairs of a vast convention center, or a weekend in the rain with few, if any, customers. The satisfaction comes from a full wallet at the end of a tiring, but productive weekend. Then the drive home is fun!

To achieve that feeling, another reality must also be faced. Craftspeople are uniquely independent and, while we may share our experiences and volunteer our assistance on a weekly basis within the closed circle of our industry, we also never forget that we are competing with each other every weekend, on a year-round basis.

During our early years in the business, my wife and I learned most lessons the hard way. It is our hope that this book will save you a great deal of the time and money we lost. It can, if you are open to adopting the philosophy and attitude we recommend and applying the lessons we share. It is especially vital for all would-be craftspeople who are starting on their journey. Our hope is that the journey Judy and I took will encourage—not discourage—you from pursuing a similarly gratifying career. If by chapter 3 you have become discouraged, turn quickly to the epilogue. But, if you need such a boost, maybe you don't have what it takes to succeed.

You should also be aware that we acknowledge and honor the independent streak that we in the crafts business possess. We know it might sometimes inhibit the reader's openness to advice and cause her to take a "Who are you?" and "What are your credentials?" attitude. Hopefully, a little background about us, presented in the first chapter, will answer those questions to your satisfaction.

I will not pretend that we can provide all the answers to every problem you will encounter as you produce and sell your merchandise. Some questions or concerns you have may be exclusive to specific crafts, and you no doubt will experience circumstances and problems that even we, after seventeen years, never ran across. However, I do believe that in this book we treat—both generally and specifically—all the major and minor areas of the business in which you will engage. If you learn to deal with them, you will be well prepared to handle other circumstances that no one can anticipate. You will also be much further down the road to developing a successful business. Remember these words!

> The right merchant is one who has the just average of faculties we call common sense; a man of a strong affinity for facts, who makes up his decision on what he has seen. He is thoroughly persuaded of the truths of arithmetic. There is always a reason, in the man, for his good or bad fortune . . . in making money. Men talk as if there were some magic about this . . . He knows that all goes on the old road, pound for pound, cent for cent—for every effect a perfect cause— and that good luck is another name for tenacity of purpose."
>
> —*Ralph Waldo Emerson*

1

A Little about the Three Basketeers

EIGHTEEN YEARS AGO, LIVING IN THE MOUNTAINS WITH THE snow piled high, Judy lined a few wicker baskets to give to friends as gifts. One couple was so impressed with Judy's talent that they invited us to share a booth in a one-day Oktoberfest in Murphys, California. Bob made nice cutting boards, as a hobby. We split a $35 booth fee, stood up two saw horses, threw a piece of plywood across them, slapped on a tablecloth, and put out our merchandise. Judy and I displayed about twenty baskets, earned $235, patted ourselves on the back and I said, "What an easy way to occasionally supplement my retirement income."

With that naïve idea in mind, the following summer, on July 4, 1982—my birthday—we tried our hand once again at a two-day show in Arnold, California. Unable to find sufficient wicker baskets, I designed a wooden, slatted picnic basket and a small breadbasket. We set up the same plywood table, covered with the same old tablecloth, and without even a canopy over our heads, were in business.

As luck would have it, it began raining just after we had set up, so I ran to a hardware store, bought a roll of black plastic and covered everything. I guess it made people just that much more curious. Like a feeding frenzy, customers scrambled under the plastic and bought almost every basket we had. I don't recommend depending on rain as a sales technique, but that day it worked. I think we displayed some thirty baskets that Judy had lined with scrap material my mother had found at Goodwill. We sold out on Sunday, grossing about $500. That was almost all profit. What a simple, easy way to make money, I thought, and stupidly made the statement, "If I can make $500 every weekend, I'll make baskets all day." I didn't know how prophetic that would be. For the next seventeen years, I was always working on my birthday!

During our first few years, we worked only small, local shows. We hit every nearby town, small club, and church event. The first time we grossed $1,000, we were ecstatic, thinking we were making big money. Then we "graduated" to the Big Time. We added to our product line and improved our skills. Our inventory grew, as did our bills. Traveling more often and further, making more baskets, we needed and purchased bigger and better vehicles and equipment. We made more money and, of course, wanted and needed more. As the saying goes, we were "in for a penny, in for a pound."

Harvest Festival shows, complete with costume; Country Folk Art exhibitions; Art and Wine festivals all over the state; street fairs; we did them all— and sometimes lost money in the process. We took whatever advice we were offered, but scattered bits of information cannot generate immediate success. As beginners, we were not fully capitalized to sustain the cost. We learned that there is an inevitable trial and error process that is expensive. We would have made a lot more money, a lot earlier, if we knew then what we know now.

As we learned, we sometimes speculated on whether our organizational and creative abilities were a blessing or a trap. Probably they were both. Our youngest son grew up surrounded by the business. He made a lot of spending money, but it probably didn't compensate for the tedium and boredom of long hours on the road and thirty shows a year. We doubt if his future wife will ever be able to drag him to a craft show.

Over the span of our career, I guess we did approximately five hundred shows. At some of them, we weren't sure that we weren't taking part in a carnival or a circus. Through all those shows, I doubt if there were many setups or teardowns, during which, at some point, Judy and I didn't have a disagreement or debate, often over the exact same thing we had discussed the week before. We listened to many a neighbor's arguments, and noted that some marriages didn't survive. If you're single, you can swear at yourself. If you have a partner, you'll need to decide on each person's duties and responsibilities. I doubt if I ever satisfactorily placed a basket on a shelf where my wife wanted it. She invariably moved it to another spot.

The crafts business is a true test of any partnership. We were successful because we learned our appropriate roles and, more important, respected each other. Judy is a "people person," who possesses the enviable quality of smiling at adversity. I am more likely to get aggravated and my charm is singularly lacking during the early morning hours, during hectic selling periods, or under strict time constraints. Hell! I'm just not charming, so I made the coffee runs!

Judy and I survived it all and retired this year with enough in the bank to secure our remaining years. Planning for your future is something we will deal with later in the book, including when it may be best to consider leaving the business. The crafts business exacts a physical and mental toll. It is not the casual, laissez-faire adventure it was when we began. Today, the little mom-and-pop booths doing a few shows a year and from whom you may purchase some specialty items are relatively rare. The business is now a highly competitive enterprise throughout the nation and much of the world. It is a billion-dollar industry. That is the arena in which you must be prepared to operate if you expect to make big money. So let's get on with learning how to compete successfully in that environment.

There is a market for any product that you as the craftsperson or artist manufacture well. As in fiction writing, where there really are no new plots—only variations on basic themes—so too in the crafts business. There are few crafts that someone else hasn't created or isn't already selling successfully. With thousands upon thousands of craftspeople throughout the country, that fact is inevitable and one to which you will just have to adjust. Later in the book, we will give you some examples of how we dealt with that reality when we were confronted with it.

The Three Basketeers was a successful business, not because there weren't other baskets on the market. There certainly were! Our business was profitable because we gave a new spin to an old standby. Our goal was to create baskets that people felt they wanted, needed, and couldn't live without. We created them to be beautiful and decorative, but also useful and functional and sturdy.

From the outset, The Three Basketeers emphasized uniqueness and attempted to personalize every item we sold. Nothing we produced was mass-produced or purchased ready-made, then simply embellished by us. You will see much of this at any show in which you compete, as you will also see many products produced overseas and therefore selling at a cheaper price than can possibly be asked, if they were manufactured in the United States. Get used to it! That is the competitive nature of the business.

However, in conscientiously sticking to our own philosophy, we created an image that became "The Three Basketeers." If you take just that one bit of advice to heart—giving the customer something unique, and giving her as much value for her money as possible, year in and year out—you'll find there is a big, money-making market for you.

2

Marketing Yourself and Your Product

THE SUBJECT OF MARKETING, FOR THOSE MAJORING IN business, constitutes many individual courses. At the corporate level, experts with degrees in sales and advertising are hired to promote and merchandise a product, and they're fired when they do not produce revenue that satisfies directors and investors.

What You Are Not

You, as a craftsperson, are not a huge corporation. You are not Kellogg's or General Motors or Microsoft, competing twenty-four hours a day with like competitors for a share of the market. You are not selling millions of dollars worth of a product and usually cannot absorb the losses, as can a large business. Unlike a big business, you cannot afford to produce inventory that does not sell and then write it off as a loss. Most often, you do not have a financial consultant at hand to save you money.

A craftsperson must adjust to surviving independent of assistance. You do not have at your disposal an entire division staffed with college-educated professionals, trained in the latest techniques necessary to sell a product. You do not have a budget for advertising on billboards, magazines, newspapers, radio, and television. You do not have a supervisor to teach and coach you as you take your first business steps. You do not have twenty-four hours a day, seven days a week to sell your product. You do not have a huge distribution center to market your product throughout the countryside. You have only you, your product, and a few days a week to convince potential customers that they want what you have to sell. To sell successfully therefore, you have to first learn what you *do* have at your disposal to sell—first your product and then yourself.

The Need to Develop Self-Reliance

What you are *not* is emphasized above to help you focus on one basic principle, relying on yourself. Most well-capitalized businesses can financially sustain some mistakes while developing and expanding. They have the experts in manufacturing, sales, and advertising to do so. Your success in the crafts business depends solely on your ability not only to produce an excellent product, but to sell it. Unless you have large monetary reserves, you must learn quickly. Nobody else is going to do it for you and very few people are going to teach you. Your success will depend primarily on your belief in your product and in yourself.

When Judy and I began, neither of us had had the slightest training in any aspect of selling or marketing. Judy had an edge, as her personality lent itself to dealing cheerfully with people. It took me at least a year to understand that I also had to cultivate her natural talent. While I was a self-reliant person, I had little confidence that our new product could really sell and even less that I had any selling ability. I had to learn to develop this trait, realizing that it was essential to moving our product off the shelf and into the customer's home. We both learned a key lesson: At the same time that we were selling our baskets, we were also selling our individuality.

Judy and I quickly noted that selling ourselves was not a matter of turning on a phony smile at a moment's notice. It was about learning and practicing ongoing, pleasant, social interaction with the public. We imitated Jim and Fran Seeley, who did this from the moment the first person passed their booth until the last customer left the show site at the end of the day. From them, Judy and I learned that when we were not actively involved with the customer and the product at the same time, we were selling little or nothing.

From a competitive standpoint, skills needed in the area of marketing must be developed quickly. Every promoter with whom I discussed the issue agreed that new people coming into the business are more experienced at marketing themselves and have more familiarity with the business skills necessary to do so. As Rhonda Blakely, a member of the family that owns and promotes Country Folk Art, expressed it, "Artisans who are changing their product, coming up with new and fresh ideas, are the people who are reporting increased business." That means that if you are a veteran and are still working on a hit-or-miss basis, the new competition is going to drive you out of business unless you develop new, improved products and better marketing techniques. If you are new to the craft world, you cannot afford to spend years learning these techniques the hard way, little by little, as Judy and I did.

Naming Your Business

One of the least considered aspects of marketing your craft and yourself that we first encountered was naming our business. This can seem inconsequential and you may ask, "What does that have to do with me and my product?" Surprisingly, a great deal more than most people realize or stop to consider. Name recognition is paramount in creating a product and a business from which to sell it. Establishing a name that everyone knows is most, if not all, of the game in which advertising engages.

The name of your business defines who you are to the public, to the promoter, to other craftspeople, and even to yourself. The name you select can intrigue a promoter if he has never seen your work before. Your sign can attract potential customers as they walk by your booth. Your business name can define you and set the stage for sales, and it can provide a means of being remembered—or forgotten. It is a vital form of marketing.

At our first few shows, we never thought of giving ourselves a name and we immediately encountered our first major problem. To whom should the buyer make out a check? So we quickly came up with the name Sew Crafty. We used it for about a year, though we recognized that it was a little too cute. We also discovered that the name was being used by many others in the business. So, living in the mountains, we became Mountain Creations. Better, but not much!

As luck would have it, six months later, we learned that another business in our county was already registered under that name and threatened to sue us if we didn't change it. We did not know that there was a state agency with which a business name could be checked and should be registered. For the second time, we had to change all our checking accounts, business cards, signs, and everything else on which we used our business name.

Finding another name became a problem. Luckily, we had imaginative friends. Doing our first Harvest Festival show, produced by one of the bigger and better promoters of craft shows, we were required to wear costumes. This is another way to advertise yourself and to stand out. Just by happenstance, our young son Mark was reading *The Three Musketeers*. The book gave us the idea of using Musketeer costumes, causing a friend to suggest that we name the business, The Three Basketeers. The name stuck and identified us throughout all the years we sold our baskets. It had that catchy quality that appeals to customers. It was easy to remember, always sparked lively conversation, gave us a logo (a plume) for our banner and business cards, and thereby enhanced the sale of our baskets in many ways.

The image you present to the public contributes immeasurably to how well you will sell your product. You probably have attended many craft shows where most of the booths looked like they belonged at a flea market and their proprietors looked equally seedy. Booth design and your overall appearance will be covered extensively in later chapters. Here, we will treat the more subtle symbols that help you appear professional and contribute to marketing yourself and your product.

Your Personal Appearance

The first thing a customer sees as she enters your booth is you. Your appearance, even before any conversational exchange takes place, is extremely important. How you present yourself physically and verbally to the customer—the first impression you make—can make the difference between a sale and no sale.

Yes, we realize that today there is a tendency to try not to judge people by their looks and appearance, and, yes, I know this is the era of casual Fridays, even at IBM, but that doesn't change reality. One of the wealthiest women I ever knew, heiress to one of the largest fortunes in the United States, dressed like a slob. Fine! She could afford the eccentricity. You can't!

A craft show certainly doesn't require formal attire and your customers may look like they walked out of a rummage sale, but you shouldn't. Looking like a throwback to the sixties or a homeless person begging on a street corner is not going to inspire confidence in you or your product. Nor is it going to help you develop a rapport with your potential customers. Certainly dress casually, but cleanly and neatly. Customers definitely do notice. It also makes you feel better about yourself.

Your Business Card

Seemingly a small item, business cards make an important contribution to sales and provide assistance in selling your product. Have them from the first day you open your booth to the public. First, business cards create the appearance of professionalism by sending the message that you are a serious business person. Many customers enter the booth, look around, and start to walk out. Don't try to detain them. Just thank them for dropping in and give them a card. Display the cards in a holder on your table. Some people will enter your booth, take a card, never look at your craft or say a word to you, and walk out. Children also like to collect them, but that's the price of doing business.

The main thing to remember is that business cards are a form of advertising. Often, having your card in their possession reminds customers of you and your product. They will often return to look again and maybe buy something. Many customers who regularly attend craft shows will keep your card as a reminder to look for your booth when they next attend a craft show.

The business card also enables customers to phone you and make a purchase after the show is over. Much of our business was generated this way. Sometimes people are not financially prepared to buy on a particular day. Sometimes the customer simply doesn't see anything that she wants right away.

Then, when she gets home, she wishes she had purchased your product. Or, a few weeks later, she needs a gift for some special occasion and your card reminds her of you. So, if the customer does make a purchase, place your business card inside the bag in which you package the purchase. Spend the extra money to have a special card designed, one of good quality and with your logo on it. It definitely makes an impression!

The Most Trivial Things Can Be Important

There are two additional things that contribute to the aura of professionalism that you must try to create. They may seem trivial, but they are essential to the way in which your customers perceive you. The first is having something in which to package the customer's purchase. The second is a schedule of the craft shows in which you will be participating that year. In both cases you are marketing yourself and your business, and establishing your professionalism.

To be sure, there are many crafts that are simply too large to be wrapped or packaged in any way. Some are also too bulky and heavy or awkward. If your craft puts you in that category, find some way to help the customer transport it to her car, if at all possible. This is particularly necessary on a rainy day. If assisting the customer in this way is not feasible, offer to store her purchase for her until she is ready to leave the show. That way, the customer doesn't have to lug it around all day.

Admittedly, this can be inconvenient when you are working in very cramped space, but assisting the customer in this way makes it worth your personal inconvenience. Often, too, when the customer returns later in the day to pick up her purchase, she may decide to buy something else. Rich Burleigh, whose promotion company is called Fire on the Mountain, told me that when he selects booths for his show, he also evaluates the craftsperson. He chooses people who subscribe to the idea of "doing it right." He calls it, "The merging of the spontaneous with the organized."

One word of caution here, though: Don't, under any circumstances, hold anything for anybody who hasn't paid for it. In the crafts business, customers who make this request are members of what are called the "Be Back Family." "I'll be back," "We'll be back," "She'll be back." They never are! They see something else they like, somewhere else, spend their money, and they are gone. Meanwhile, you have lost the ability to sell that particular piece of merchandise, perhaps for the entire day.

Your Craft Show Schedule

The show schedule I mentioned above can contribute immeasurably to your sales for the remainder of the year. Everyone who enters your booth should be given your schedule. This is especially important at street fairs, where customers have not paid to enter the show. They may be out for a Sunday walk and haven't brought enough money with them to buy. Or, before they even entered your booth, they may simply have spent all the money they had or intended to spend that day. The schedule tells them when and where you will be in the future. The schedule also provides them with your telephone number should they want to order by phone. You can develop, as we did, a very large customer base in this manner. A show schedule constitutes advertising, marketing, and good public relations all at the same time.

Along these same lines, many of the big, traveling shows—like Harvest Festival and Country Folk Art—will mail you, on your acceptance to the show, a stack of cards. These cards usually offer an entry-fee discount and include the promoters' upcoming show schedule. You should place them in a conspicuous place on your counter at every show you do. Give them to everyone who enters your booth, whether they make a purchase or not. Drop them in the bag with every customer purchase. It is amazing how many people want that dollar off. They will thank you for the card and show up at that next show to buy at your booth. We had a rubber stamp with our business name and logo that we applied to every promoter's card. We would check the shows we were going to participate in. That card would act as an advertisement for both our business and for the particular promoter's upcoming shows.

The Importance of a Large Inventory to Your Sales

The next lesson that we learned was that it is essential that you have sufficient inventory. To an extent, this will also be discussed in more detail under the chapter on booth setup and display. It is, however, relevant here because customers want a large selection from which to choose. Sufficient selection of merchandise gives you greater sales potential, more with which to keep the customer in the booth.

As a novice, it is very difficult to judge just how much of your product you should bring to a show. Yet, many veteran craftspeople also neglect this area of their business. Of course, anyone may be limited by his own cash reserve and how much inventory he can afford to stock and have the physical capacity to produce. But, beyond that, there is a natural tendency to take too little simply because, to you, it looks like a lot.

Since you may not have ever produced in volume before, the amount of inventory to bring to a show is difficult to judge. Just how much is too much and how much is too little is a matter of trial and error but, because too little can drastically affect your sales ability, it is better to err on the side of too much.

This inventory predicament happened to Judy and me for the first two years we were in business. When we began, we displayed a total of perhaps thirty or forty baskets of three different designs and we usually sold out, but we weren't making much money. Then, as we expanded our variety, we set ten of each basket as our target for each show. What took time to realize, however, was that once we had sold five or six of each, we had sold the most desirable of our baskets and we had no selection left with which to entice the customer. The booth looked empty and that fact alone may discourage customers.

A virtually empty booth, no matter how fine your product, still looks a bit bare. Nobody wants what they consider leftovers. As a salesperson, no matter how good your sales ability, with nothing to sell, you might as well not be at the show. To experienced customers, an empty booth makes a poor impression.

Experienced customers know when the best merchandise has been taken and their perception of you as a craftsperson is that you have nothing much to offer. Furthermore, since our sale of baskets depended on color schemes and color coordination—something on which your product may well rely—if we had only a scant selection from which to choose, there was nothing to discuss with the customer. We couldn't sell ourselves and we couldn't sell our product. Or, as Rhonda Blakely of Country Folk Art aptly noted, "You can't sell from an empty wagon." She and her family have been promoting shows for eighteen years—fifty shows a year, from the Atlantic to the Pacific coast—so she knows. As a general rule, many craftspeople work on the principle that at good shows, you should sell half of what you bring to the show. Obviously, then, you can't start with an "empty wagon" if you are going to make money.

To sell correctly, we realized that if we wanted to make big money, we had to make it a full-time enterprise. Thereafter, we never stocked our booth with less than thirty and often forty or fifty of our bestselling baskets and half as many of the less popular, but still reliable sellers. Judy convinced me, and she was correct, that the more we took, the more we sold. We had lots to sell and a lot to talk about.

The Reality of the Craft Marketplace

From the beginning of our craft show venture, and regularly throughout, Judy and I reminded each other of one basic reality that can keep you humble, keep you productively creative, and keep your business life in perspective: Nobody needs what any craftsperson has to sell. That is a hard reality to face, but if you are too egocentrically involved in your craft and are unable to admit and acknowledge it, you won't be able to sell or market your craft successfully, and, inevitably, you will lose money.

To have a good grasp of this core reality, you must bury your artistic ego. The truth is that crafts, like most commodities, appeal primarily to a customer's wishes, desires, and fantasies. It is not far-fetched to say that the entire business and advertising world is based on understanding that fact. As a craftsperson, it is your goal, in attracting customers, to capitalize on your awareness of that fact and convince the customer that your product fulfills those dreams and fantasies.

Now you may never have considered this, but it is true: Most people who come to a craft show do not know what they want to buy. They usually walk around looking and waiting for that special something to "speak to them." Most often, they know that they would like to buy something, if they can find something that fits into their budget and appeals to them. Your product has to be that special something that tempts them to reach into their wallet and part with their hard-earned money.

It is important to remember that term, *hard-earned*. As you meet and observe your crafts competitors, you will be surprised at how many, during the course of the day, develop a resentful attitude when people are not spending their money. They seem to think that just because they have expended the effort to be at the show, the patron has some obligation to make a purchase. When a customer leaves the booth without buying, far too many crafts merchants act as if they had been personally insulted and become surly. They allow the customer's failure to make a purchase to affect their mood for the remainder of the day and thereby lose even more sales. So, if you find yourself taking that attitude, get rid of it. It will not help you to sell yourself or your craft.

A good way to evaluate yourself and your product, and to understand potential customers, is to ask yourself this question: Would I buy this? It is a simple, but sometimes very scary, question. Many, perhaps most, craftspeople never ask this question of themselves, because they wouldn't like the answer. As Judy and I learned to ask that question—and as we remembered to keep it in focus throughout our career, particularly when we designed a new basket—we began to engage in a ritual at every show that enabled us to evaluate the competition and our own product. This ritual provided insight into what we could anticipate over the next few days, which, in turn helped us to maintain our composure and selling ability.

Before every show opened, one or both of us would amble up and down the rows of booths. Predictably, we would see what we came to refer to as Foo-Foo. There would be three or four vendors selling stuffed dolls, two or three selling dried flowers, another couple with a booth full of wooden stakes with cutesy-pie sayings and mottoes, a number with miniature ceramic figurines, junk jewelry, and the like. Then there would be five booths filled with birdhouses, six different potters, and numerous people selling reprints of their artwork, some with a conglomeration of a little of everything.

Cynical as it may sound, that was great for us. We knew that too many merchants were going to be competing with the same products, for the same customers. Since nobody sold a product like ours, because we created it, we knew we would get more than our share of the market. Of course, frequently there were other kinds of baskets, but none that were in competition with ours. Maybe nobody really needed our baskets, but if they desired one, we usually had a corner on the potential market.

On completing our walk, we immediately knew three things: If we treated every customer with courtesy and respect, our product was going to sell. We knew that, regardless of any adversity, we were going to make a good profit. And we knew we could count on hearing a lot of complaining about what a poor show it had been from those who didn't earn as much money as we did.

Later in the book, you will find a list of excuses and alibis that craftspeople regularly use to justify their lack of sales. However, if you are confident about your product and your ability to sell it, when you're having that inevitable bad day, you'll resist the temptation to use them. If you are producing a good product and selling your unique personality to the customer, the "bad days" will become less frequent. You won't need the excuses. Rationalizations may satisfy the ego temporarily, but they don't put money in your pocket. The mental energy expended in creating phony excuses engenders a negative attitude that hampers your salesmanship and can ruin what might have become a good day.

That term, a *good day*, leads to discussion of another problem that can affect your ability to sell: Except at very rare shows, for very specific reasons, most days start off slowly. People don't usually rush into a show and immediately start buying. Bill Campbell taught us this when I noticed that during the entire first day, he had not sold a single rocking horse. I suggested that maybe he was in the wrong area, to which he responded, "Wait until tomorrow." What Bill knew was that since he had a high-priced item, people needed to go home and think about the investment they were making. Women may buy expensive earrings on impulse, but not rocking horses. The next day Bill sold five at $750 a piece.

So don't start looking for excuses as to why your product isn't selling only a few hours after the show's opening. Give people time to look around, to think about what they truly want. We rarely sold much the first few hours, but we always went home with a good profit. If you have a good product, after they've looked at a great deal of garbage, they'll be back to your booth to buy. And you won't frustrate yourself unnecessarily.

Never Be Self-Satisfied

What I am now about to write may seem even more cynical, callous, or even greedy, but again, it is reality. As a craftsperson, as a merchant, as a vendor, or whatever you may call yourself, you must never be satisfied with the profit you are making. That attitude leads to stagnation and eventually, profit loss.

As in any endeavor, but particularly in the creation of a product, you should always believe that you can make a better product and make even more money. Possessing that attitude is a reflection of your self-confidence. That self-confidence will then naturally and almost automatically be reflected in the quality and output of your product, your continued creativity, and your attitude when selling it.

Try to Produce Something Different

Would I buy this? Whether you are an "in the cradle beginner" or "a rocking chair veteran," if your product is unique, if you believe in it, and if you are positively involved in the selling process, you should be able to truthfully answer "yes" to that question. If you can't, ask yourself whether anyone else would. If the answer is "yes," then you're on your way.

This doesn't mean that you can't produce Foo-Foo. It does mean, however, that if you want to earn more than an average living, your Foo-Foo must be better produced than anyone else's and must capture the imagination of the customer in a way that another merchant's work does not. Even so, as good as your work may be, you will still have to hope that a potential customer hasn't already spent her money at another booth like yours, somewhere down the aisle before ever seeing your workmanship. This, then, may be a good time to discuss and define the term *unique*.

In the craft world, unique doesn't necessarily mean one-of-a-kind. Every promoter with whom I discussed this issue agreed that the one-of-a-kind craft is fast disappearing, noting that the pressure to do more shows has created a need to have more products that are easier to produce in order to meet greater demand. Oh, each new craft season you may occasionally see something that you have never seen before and it may be truly one-of-a-kind, but the reality is that by next year, or maybe sooner, someone will have copied it and created his own variation. It is not uncommon, as has happened with many inventions, that more than one artisan will develop the same concept at the same time. So, *unique* really refers to the way you personalize your product and the way you display it.

Do you grow, dry, and dye your own flowers? If you're a potter, a unique approach may refer to the way you shape, color, or glaze a pot. Are your earrings distinctly different or can they be purchased at any dime store? Is your stained glass artistically individual or are your patterns and designs like everybody else's? Do you create your own clothing designs or truly different wooden shelves or merely take patterns out of a book? Many do this and make a living, but not much more than that.

Actually, one-of-a-kind is relatively rare anyway. It is found primarily in the fine arts but, even there, a painting is a painting; earrings are earrings. It is the uniqueness that the artist brings to the painting or the creation of the earring that makes it different. Most often, the one-of-a-kind piece is a gimmick item that usually doesn't survive more than a few years. What makes and sells your product as *unique*, is what you give to the product that is genuinely you, and that includes how you sell "you" to the customer as you sell your product. Promoters all agree that customers like the interaction with the artist and like to talk with and get to know the person who created what they have purchased. The personal connection is very important, especially if your product is unique.

At our first shows, Judy and I observed that, though there were other kinds of baskets in the show, ours were unlike any others made. If you can say that, you can then capitalize on that fact. Then, if you can smile at the customers, show them that you enjoy their company, you sell yourself, your product, and your entire business. Your entire operation sells itself as unique.

Try to Stand Out from the Competition

When you attend a craft show, particularly one that is outdoors, you will see row after row of canopies, all ten-by-ten feet, all virtually alike. One promoter told me laughingly that he thought that the invention of the portable, retractable canopy began the downgrading of outdoor craft presentation. Craftspeople ceased to be individual in the creation of their booth. And his point is well taken. It is not until the customer looks inside your booth that your product is defined. Once the customer steps inside, it is up to you and your product to keep her there.

So, for example, we always placed our largest and most colorful baskets at the front of the booth. We also kept a scrapbook with photos of us in every phase of production. It helped sell baskets because in crowded conditions it kept the customer interested and it verified that we made the product and that the baskets were truly original. The scrapbook was also a great conversation piece with which to break the ice.

For a few years, I wrote humorous poems that applied to every basket and gave the customer a copy with her purchase. Still another year, we designed a basket I called a Flambajobble. The name was a literary invention, but the fantasy story I told about the basket, kept customers intrigued. The Flambajobble was an intentionally weird basket and we didn't sell many. But, we sold a lot of our other baskets. While we were entertaining them, our customers were also looking around.

As noted above, it is good to remember that you yourself are an original. If your sales seem to be diminishing, look to yourself as well as your product. You must never be so wed to an idea, a product, or your image of yourself, that you are not open to modifying or changing it for the sake of product improvement and selling success.

Flexibility on your part is vital to success in the crafts game. That is why each year Judy and I created new baskets and discarded nonsellers from the previous year. One year we designed five new baskets and dropped four of them by July. We loved some of those baskets, but they didn't sell. The inability of so many craftspeople to part with their creations, and so continue to sell the exact same product year after year, explains why so many of them either go out of business or just eke out a living.

Are there exceptions? Definitely! A good friend has been making large women's purses for twenty years. She has varied the basic style, pattern, or color very little. However, they are practical, durable, and washable. Nobody makes a purse the way she does and nobody has tried. Since all women have numerous purses for various occasions, Jessie's purses will always be desired and useful. Little girls, who once attended shows with their mothers, grew up and bought Jessie's purse. She has always had a market and always will.

Variety Is the Spice of Life

Success depends on what you are selling and how good your products are. Our customers would never need more than one sewing or picnic basket. Over the years they might buy one for friends and relatives, but we couldn't make a living just selling those two baskets. We had to develop many kinds of baskets. All were functional and utilitarian.

This constant process of invention and reinvention is an agonizing, personal process. We thought that many, maybe all of our baskets, were beautiful and useful. But, a craft booth is not a museum to which you are charging admission. I can't remember all the baskets we created and discarded. Since they didn't sell, they were worthless. We ate our losses and created something new. This approach generated the repeat business that made for our success. Henry Ford could not sell his Model T—today!

However, we tried to make the loss worthwhile. When a basket wasn't selling, we made it a practice to ask customers what they didn't like about it. We solicited their ideas and redesigned accordingly. The idea for a number of our baskets came from someone with a particular need. We had designed a jewelry tray that we thought was very pretty. It didn't sell. Then one day a customer picked it up and pointed out that, slightly enlarged and with two dividers, it would make a beautiful utensil tray for outdoor picnics and barbecues. We made the change and over the years we must have sold a few thousand.

Whenever that happened, if the basket turned out to be a financial success, we sent the customer who had suggested it a free basket as a thank you. The customers appreciated that and kept coming back year after year—and made more useful suggestions.

Creating something unique and being able to market it successfully by applying the above approach has another advantage: There is nothing you can produce that someone else can't imitate. But the act of creating your product and doing variations on your own basic theme gives you a selling advantage. Let me give you an example.

The Copycat

One year a vendor next to us watched us have a big payday. Of the twenty different baskets we displayed, this day we were selling dozens of one particular style. His booth was an accumulation of other people's ideas and he was having a particularly bad year. Under financial pressure, he decided to copy and produce this one basket, hoping to make a lot of money selling our creation the remainder of the year. Forgetting his lack of ethics, he also forgot that we participated in many of the same shows.

Now, there is a phenomenon that takes place at craft shows that none of us in the business has ever been able to fully explain. On any given day, at any given location, for reasons completely unfathomable, every customer is attracted to the same item in your booth. Maybe it is simply that one customer sees another customer attracted to an item and so, having confirmation of her taste, she buys it. This can be contagious. Over the years, this basket had been a consistent seller, but never like this day. Copycat didn't know that.

About six months later, at another show, Copycat approached me and apologized. He had produced twenty of these baskets and hadn't sold one. He didn't sell them because he didn't have our experience, reputation, or variety in his booth. He had them displayed next to some cowboy boot birdhouses. That basket sold for us because it was utilitarian. As a matter of fact, it was designed as a basket to hold French bread. A customer, having gone home and measured it, found that it happened to fit exactly on the tank of the standard toilet bowl. From that day on, the French breadbasket also became a basket to hold toilet paper and a tissue box. The result was that we also had some funny stories to tell our customers about it. Copycat knew none of this. I accepted his apology, but I wasn't about to buy up his stock. I also didn't tell him why he couldn't sell them.

There are many people in the business—veterans and novices—who have no real talent or creativity. That they make a living is all that can be said for them. Frankly, they are an asset to those who have talent. They fill up spaces at a craft show and, if you're good, you look even better by comparison. If that sounds a little too cynical, it is intentional.

The crafts business is as competitive as any other business, maybe more so. You have to decide if you want to just fill up the promoter's space or make money.

Know Yourself, Your Assets, and Your Limitations

Now, reading this, you may be saying to yourself, "I'm not sure that I am as talented as necessary, as imaginative, or as competitive." Well, definitely a certain amount of self-questioning and -examination is natural, actually good. That should be part of the process when you enter the business and throughout your career. Judy is an optimist; I'm a pessimist, so I was particularly dubious about many things. Judy and I had no idea how successful we could be when we started. We are, however, both "stick-to-it" type people.

My knowledge of woodworking did not extend beyond the use of a hammer, saw, screwdriver, and jigsaw. Thousands of men and women are better woodworkers than I am. Judy owned a small sewing machine that she hadn't used regularly for years. She had little more than basic knowledge or experience about sewing as a craft. Little by little, we added equipment as we learned to use it and as we enlarged our product line.

The point is, you're probably more creative and capable of manufacturing and selling than you think. Creativity is rarely a spontaneous inspiration or a miraculous revelation. More often, creativity and salesmanship develop as a tiny seed, a germ of an idea that grows with nourishment. That nourishment is the practical use of your eyes, your ears, and your brain. Then you have to put into action what you have been taught.

To create something unique, you do not have to be an artistic genius. You are a craftsperson, maybe even an artist at your craft, but you are also a vendor, a peddler, a traveling salesperson. Some people don't like those terms and even resent them, but to one degree or another, they still apply to people in the business.

Your goal in the business is making money. Your product must be durable: It should not fall apart before the customer leaves the building or parking lot, and we've seen that happen. But, you are also not creating and selling to museums. As Beth Weber, a promoter, pointed out to me, "Over the years the craftspeople who remained in the business were those who 'got better and better' with experience." Beth also thought that this fact helped to rid the crafts business of its "flea market image." She was concerned that newcomers to the crafts industry seemed to be "less concerned" with quality and perhaps placed too much emphasis on making money. And she was right! Money is the goal, certainly, but you must put care and attention into the means of acquiring it.

Another promoter pointed out the reality of decreased attendance at craft shows over the past ten years. Craftspeople are now not just competing with others in the crafts business. They are competing with other craft shows on the same weekend. The malls and warehouse stores carry variations on products once almost exclusively found at craft shows. Many have created venues within their stores to resemble the craft show atmosphere and ambiance. Mail-order catalogues have cut into the craftsperson's retail business. The result is that in order to compete successfully, your goal—to earn a substantial living—must be first to produce a substantial product and then fully market yourself and that product. Do that and the money will come.

Reevaluate the Crafts Business

Go to any craft show. You've probably already been to dozens or you wouldn't be thinking of going into the business. If you're already in the business, go to your next show with a new eye, a different perspective. Look at every booth in the show and see how many are producing basically the same product, with a few different wrinkles.

For example, suppose you make pretty, dried-flower arrangements for wall display. Your friends have told you how beautiful they are. Well, there are probably at least a few hundred craft merchants selling such arrangements in California alone, and some of them will be at any show in which you participate. So, you immediately face competition with far more experience than you do, if you are a beginner.

Now, face financial reality. Even at well-attended shows, there is just so much money in people's pockets. Every person is not your potential customer. You want your share of those who are looking for something to cover a space on their wall. The key to that is in your product. If you can develop a dried-flower arrangement that the buying public doesn't see everywhere, you will stand out from the competition. If you're planning to produce or are already selling a well-established craft, no better or different than anybody else's, reevaluate yourself and your product. If it's being done, it's probably already being done better than you can do it. However, if you're convinced you're dried-flower arrangement is truly different, go for it, but be prepared for the competition.

Some customers walk an entire show, making a list of booths that interest them, before they ever make a purchase. Still others, on impulse, will buy the first thing that they see and like. You can't do anything about that. If they see another potter, on another aisle, before they get to you, you may miss that potential customer. Your location at a show may also reduce your chances for sales. Except under special circumstances, to be explained later, you can't do much about that either. It's the luck of the draw. So observe and then change the things you can do something about—your craft and yourself.

Set Your Standard High

From your first show as a beginner or, if you are a veteran beginning next weekend, make it your primary goal to establish a reputation for quality and excellence in your product. Ask yourself these questions: Did I make my product of the highest-quality materials available? Will the customer be happy to put it in her home? Would I put it in my home? Did the customer leave the booth with a lasting, positive impression, whether she made a purchase or not? Are customers likely to recommend me to their friends? Will the customer return?

Initially, Judy and I didn't recognize that the answers to the above questions involved marketing and selling. We thought it sufficient to aim for a quality product, thinking the baskets would sell themselves. Not so! You will lose money allowing a product to sell itself. What we discovered was that most customers at a craft show are not impulse buyers. They are very discerning and, according to promoters, becoming more so, particularly when they are paying an admission price to enter the show in the first place. They don't come just to look, another promoter pointed out. They may buy cheap knickknacks on impulse, but most spend their money carefully and examine a product with a cautious eye. Those were the customers who came back looking for us year after year and those are the customers you want to cultivate through the standards you set for yourself, the quality of the product you produce, and, as a result, the reputation you achieve.

Keep Up with the Trends, Fads, and Even Eccentricities of Your Public

As you develop your product and create a demand for it, you should also be researching the latest trends as they may apply to your craft. That doesn't mean you should fall into line with every fad. But, you want to keep up, for instance, with what color schemes are currently popular, still making sure you have enough variety to appeal to every taste.

Trends are playing an increasingly important role in the crafts business. They are changing more rapidly now. As the crafts business expands nationally, as there are more and more arts and craft shows, and as more people enter the field, the demand to produce more products is leading to mass production. Mass production can quickly bore the buying public because it uses up new ideas at a faster rate, which, in turn, leads to a need to be more and more creative, and generates a new demand. In essence, you can't sell what people don't want.

We had a customer we called the Lavender Lady. She dressed from hat to shoes in lavender. Even her cat was clothed in lavender. Eccentric yes, but with a very big lavender purse. Every year we made sure to have one of every new basket in lavender. We set them aside for her. Then we'd pray she would show up or we were stuck with those lavender baskets for the year. Almost nobody likes lavender—or canary yellow for that matter.

We took a gamble, but it was well worth it. The Lavender Lady never failed us. One year she picked up our $50 picnic basket, put the cat in it, and paid happily. I was even happier! We sure couldn't sell the basket to anyone else after the cat had been in it! However, the loss would still have been slight, because the Lavender Lady had lots of friends she brought along with her. They turned out to be the regular customers with whom we did a continuing, repeat business for many years. Keeping up with one customer's desires gained us many more, each with her own particular taste.

That is the essence of selling yourself and your product. Selling your craft is not just how much inventory you move or how much money you make today.

Marketing is about building a reputation for quality and friendliness that brings your customers back to you repeatedly. The latest fad—the craft item that suddenly appears—is something over which you have no control. For a time, it may seem to be taking money out of your pocket. The guy who sells a baseball hat with a propeller on top may be very annoying when you watch him raking in the cash while you have a rotten day. The person who sells out of some trash item, while you, with a unique, high-quality product to which you have devoted endless artistic effort, sell very little, can engender feelings of envy. But mostly, the sellers of tawdry, whimsical items will not be in business long and do not hurt you in the long run. You must, however, be conscious of trends, particularly if they relate to colors, fashions, and furniture—anything that will have a fairly long-lasting effect on your business. You may still see a few people around selling tie-dyed T-shirts, but not many and not making much money. Your T-shirts had better have some different saying on them and be fashionably up-to-date. At first, our baskets were ultracountry, but as trends and tastes changed, we gave them an updated look in color and design.

Continue Evaluating Yourself

Assuming you are convinced that you have a great, marketable product that can produce a good living, the next thing you have to do is evaluate yourself once again. This may be more difficult than evaluating your craft. It is perhaps the most difficult thing we all have to do in life.

The crafts business is just a microcosm of the larger world. We have discussed many marketing and sales techniques needed to succeed financially. But, have you considered and assessed the pros and cons of your own personality in relation to the crafts business? Can you face them honestly and then change those things about yourself in order to substantially improve your income potential? To help yourself figure this out, ask yourself these questions:

How committed am I? How hard am I willing to work? Will I or do I enjoy a gypsy lifestyle? If I don't, can I adjust to it, and for how long? Do I enjoy people? Can my physical and mental health sustain long hours, physically demanding effort, and a frantic pace? Am I capable of maintaining the necessary positive frame of mind? How long, based on my previous experience, can I sustain my ambition? Am I likely to quit when the business gets tough or am I a fighter? How long do I generate enthusiasm? Am I quickly bored? Knowing the honest answers to these questions is vital to marketing yourself as well as your product.

As acknowledged in the introduction, Judy and I just stumbled into the business and never considered these questions in relation to selling. Most craftspeople we met never did until they were deeply involved in the business. Sometimes, by then it is too late. We were simply lucky, as we were older, had experienced other professions, and knew our capabilities. We had never dodged hard work and had proven to ourselves that we had the tenacity to stick to it and make the necessary adjustments. Do you? For, once you make the financial commitment, you have no choice but to be dedicated. And, once you've made the financial commitment, you may find that you still are not able to generate the necessary energy. Try to avoid such a forced choice. Know your strengths *and* your limitations.

Travel, for example, is wearing and time consuming. Maybe you hate motels. If that's the case, reevaluate your show schedule. You may be in a rut, doing the same shows year after year out of habit, but not necessarily because they generate the most net income. Such circumstances can impact negatively on your selling ability.

Pay attention to the pressures under which you are selling yourself and your product. How is it affecting you? Among serious professionals in the business, unless you do at least twenty shows a year, you're considered a dilettante. That doesn't mean you should start by doing that many shows. To the contrary, our recommendation if you are new to the business is to schedule no more than ten shows the first year, possibly fewer. Selection of craft shows is addressed in chapter 5, but I mention it here because it is important as you evaluate yourself.

The first year, you need the time to analyze your product, yourself, and the shows you're participating in. Once you are doing twenty or more shows (many of us do more than thirty), you are stressed in ways you cannot foresee. That many shows require twelve-to-fifteen-hour days, seven days a week, almost fifty-two weeks a year. We rarely had more than a week's vacation a year. You will eat, sleep, and literally dream the crafts business.

That is not fun! There is nothing glamorous about the crafts business. The craft world is about making money and what you have to know and do to make it. We do not wish to discourage you with that bit of realism; we just want you to recognize the pressures that exist and the commitment you have to make sell your product successfully.

Time constraints and pressure are especially acute during the latter part of the year. Your ability to sell yourself and your product will be affected by these factors. Most of the year, you will earn enough to pay for your business expenses, cover your personal budget, and, hopefully, take in some additional profit. But, the big money is always earned during the holiday season. You must be gearing yourself and your business toward this time of year, even while preparing for next week's show. For those shows, you must produce inventory in advance, adding to the pressure under which you must produce and sell all year. The last thing you ever want to do is sell out. That means you didn't have enough inventory to sell and you lost potential income.

Friends of ours sold their entire stock of candy on the first day of a Harvest Festival show—$2,500's worth of sweets. They could not take down their booth and go home. They sat there for two days earning and producing nothing. To say they were angry and frustrated is to put it mildly. Such frustration can easily contribute to physical and mental deterioration that, in turn, can affect the quality of your product and your ability to sell it. Helen and Tom worked twice as hard the following week and were behind schedule for the remainder of the year.

We suggest that newcomers to the business do no more than ten shows their first year. And if you are a veteran who is experiencing the Law of Diminishing Returns, reduce the number of shows that you schedule. In both cases, this will allow you time to evaluate your competition, your product, and yourself. Do your bookkeeping carefully. Learn how much money you must earn to be content, creative, and productive. Test your price line. Develop your public relations skills. Practice your new selling techniques and approaches. Be consciously aware of what you are saying and doing. Start off slow, but start off right.

When the season ends, decide the degree to which you desire to continue or expand your schedule. You must determine if you can sell and market competitively at an increased rate, which means getting your share of the market. You can't produce and market your best product, or greet your customers with your best foot forward, if you're burned out creatively, frustrated, despondent, or lack enthusiasm.

During lunch hour, when business gets slow and the day is very hot, it is easy to nod off. One such day, I fell asleep in the booth while Judy was off having lunch. I was in my Musketeer costume, which made me look even more like a statue. I awoke to hear a little girl ask her mother, "Mommy, is he real or is he a dummy?" Judy returned at that moment and readily provided the answer. Luckily, the woman was interested in our product, in spite of my inattention, so we did not lose a sale, but we should have and would have, if it hadn't been for Judy. Staring into space, your mind in a netherworld, doesn't entice a customer into your booth. If you're not prepared to greet the customer with a smile, you're not prepared to sell yourself or your product.

3

Pricing Your Product

AVING ESTABLISHED WHAT YOU NEED TO DO TO SELL successfully, and assuming that you have a good product, a good variety, and that you're working hard to build your inventory, and that you've followed our every direction and subscribed to our best advice, you're probably poised to make a lot of money. Well, maybe, and maybe not.

The Difficulty of Pricing Your Craft

If there is a stumbling block in the crafts business, one that drives the most experienced craftsperson crazy, it is the pricing of your product. This may well be the most difficult, and could arguably be considered the most important aspect of your business. It is also a question for which there are no pat answers. There is no mathematical formula that you can apply to this problem.

If you hired Judy and me to come to your booth to assist you in pricing your product, after we knew your cost of production, compared it to similar products on the market and at craft shows, considered your craftsmanship and the quality and durability of your product, we could then give you a rough estimate of the price that you might charge. However, we could never give you a guarantee that that would be the best price for which the merchandise should be sold. The price we set may still be too low or too high and therefore affect your profit margin either way. For, regardless of how good your product and how charming your sales personality and technique, price your product incorrectly and you will make fewer sales and less money.

Since the subject of marketing includes anything that involves the placing of your product in front of the buying public, pricing is considered part of marketing and, as such, should possibly have been included in the previous chapter. The price you place on your craft is vital in determining whether you attract or discourage customers. Some people will enter your booth and the only thing they will really look at is the price of your merchandise. It will be their sole determinant as to whether to buy from you or not. Therefore, because of this subject's importance, it deserves a chapter of its own.

When Judy and I began our business, we not only had no idea what to charge for our baskets, but we hardly even discussed it. We knew, as should you, what it cost to produce a basket and how much time it took to complete each unit. But, how much to charge for each basket, how much profit we could fairly request—these were questions that, in our former professions, we had never had to consider. How much profit would the traffic bear? For us, it was an unknown quantity.

A Variety of Factors Affect Your Price

The fact is that there is no exact and precise answer to the quandary of pricing. Assuming that you have a wonderful product, price is still affected by the economics of the area in which you are selling. The season of the year strongly impacts and determines your income potential on any given weekend. The fall season prior to the holidays presents your biggest potential for income. After the holidays, the beginning of the year will be your slowest time, as people have spent all their money and don't want to run up their credit cards any further. However, you can't adjust and readjust according to these continual variables.

The type of customer the show is attracting will affect your weekly income. If you are in a depressed economic area, people will naturally have less money. Should a normally solid financial area have been hit by industry closings, layoffs—or, in a farm area, drought or flood—you will find that your income potential will fall off from the previous year.

Even very large, overall cultural changes will affect your pricing over a period of years. Smaller promoters cannot and needn't bother to survey this kind of information, but a large organization like Harvest Festival regularly conducts surveys in an attempt to understand and explain how changing cultural patterns may affect the way craft show customers are spending their money. Harvest Festival promoters have found, for example, that there has been a definite change in the spending behavior of what is referred to as the DINK (double income, no kids) generation. In the past, married couples would spend $500–$2,000 a year at Harvest Festival shows and could be counted on to return each year. Now that group of people is not spending as much, and may actually be disappearing as a distinct entity. It is believed that downsizing of major corporations has had an impact on these couples, since both family members may not be consistently working now. Then, too, they may simply have had children, which, obviously, drastically changes where a married couple spend their money and how much money they have left to indulge their every desire. Country Folk Art has found that while their attendance at shows has not diminished, because of oversaturation of the marketplace (too many shows in the same area), the individual customer may not be buying as much at any given show. There is always another show next week. Therefore, your pricing may be a paramount element to your success.

Even the nature of your craft will also impact your pricing scheme. Toys may be in more demand than stuffed teddy bears. In the spring, floral arrangements are going to be better sellers than Christmas ornaments and vice versa in the fall and early winter.

To the greatest extent possible, try to evaluate these factors before applying to a show in certain areas at certain times. Just because you did well last year, or even over the last five years, that is not an absolute indicator that you will make money this year. Whether it's the beginning or the end of the month and people have or have not received their pay or retirement checks may also have an impact on your sales. Income tax time may make a big difference in your sales as well.

You have to learn to try to anticipate such factors whenever possible. The way you present your product to the public is still another variable in the prices you can command, and it's something to which you must pay close attention. There will be more detail on this in chapter 7 on Booth Setup and Booth Display; however, the following is especially relevant to this subject.

The Loss Leader

There is in the retail business, a concept known as a *loss leader*. This refers to an item or items on which you are prepared to accept a minimal loss. They are used to attract customers into the store or, in this case, into your booth. They should be quick and easy to produce and particularly eye-catching. Sometimes a loss leader may be a gimmick item or a small sample of the craft you produce, or something that is very inexpensive and appeals to children, drawing their parents into the booth. And, as a matter of fact, if you select and manufacture the right product, it may not even have to be a loser. But, winner or loser, the advantage of the loss leader to your pricing is that it can give you a price measure to compare to the other items you are selling. If you are only selling your loss leader, something is usually wrong with how you are pricing the rest of your merchandise.

Very early in our career, Judy came up with the idea of selling plant stakes. We traced hearts, rabbits, bears, and other figures on our scrap wood, cut them out, decorated them, put them on a stick, and never had less than a hundred sitting in large vases at the front of the booth. We never charged more than $2 apiece for them, sometimes only a dollar if we thought that money was in short supply. Most often, we sold enough of them to pay for our booth fee. However, if all the first customers who entered the booth purchased only plant stakes, we were usually in for a bad day, which meant either that we were in a depressed economic area or our prices were off base.

A few years later, Judy suggested a very small, wooden, slatted basket with painted wooden tulips in it. Plant stakes were out and Judy thought this might be a better loss leader. I thought it was the dumbest idea she had ever had. "Who would want to buy wooden tulips?" I foolishly asked. Nevertheless, I made them. We put the basket on a shelf at the front of our booth and charged $10 for them. We sold ten the first weekend and thereafter rarely sold fewer than twenty a show, sometimes thirty or forty.

These baskets were easy to produce, requiring very little time, and were made mostly of scrap material. They were almost pure profit. Those tulip baskets became one of the mainstays of our inventory for about six years and, according to the Law of Supply and Demand, we found that we could raise the price to $20 and still sell just as many. You can be sure that Judy never failed to remind me of what I had said and you can be equally sure that I never again questioned her judgment as to what women prefer. Truthfully, I never did like the tulip baskets, but they made money, so I set aside my personal distaste for the baskets and made them.

You Can't Make Constant Price Adjustments

Unfortunately, as noted above, the one thing you cannot do is adjust your prices according to many of the variables mentioned. Too many customers travel each weekend from show to show. Today's customers will remember not only what they paid last week, but also what they were charged the year before. Nor can you test what the traffic will bear on Saturday and reduce or raise your price on Sunday. Many customers come to a show both days and you'll catch hell from somebody who paid more yesterday than you are charging today. We did that once and had to make a refund. Occasionally, perhaps yearly "cost of doing business" increases are tolerable and will be understood by your repeat customers. But, you cannot make drastic price changes from day to day or even week to week.

As with everything else in the crafts business, there is an exception. An artist friend of ours, who worked in oils, taught me this. In front of his booth he always had a very large painting that he priced at $5,000. That may seem like an unusual price for a loss leader, but in this case the goal was different. He knew, just as well as I, that virtually no one goes to a craft show to buy a $5,000 painting. If they are going to spend that much money, they'll go to a reputable, established art gallery. He never did sell that painting at a craft show, as far as I know, but he sure sold a lot of small paintings and prints. Customers looked at and admired the $5,000 painting; somehow the price established his credentials as an artist. Then they thought they were getting a bargain on anything that they did purchase.

I thought I'd try that sales technique and built a giant basket for which I charged $200. The idea didn't work for us. Two hundred dollars is a long way from $5,000. Someone bought the basket the first day of the show. That was not what I wanted. There was far too much work, time, and money involved in producing it to make it really profitable, nor did we have enough room in our truck to transport a number of such baskets. So, I never made another.

The Hourly Wage Issue

A special word of advice: Never, never, never determine your price on the basis of how much you think your work is worth on an hourly basis. There is a strong temptation to do this and you must resist it. Over the years, we cannot count the number of craftspeople with whom we discussed this issue and who tried to apply that pricing strategy and lost a lot of money or quit the business.

Sometimes, these craftspeople had worked in previous jobs that paid on an hourly-wage basis. Millions of workers do. So, when you are new to the business, this approach may seem logical. The veteran who insists on it simply hasn't done her homework or is allowing her ego to get in the way of her better judgment. This approach simply does not apply to the crafts business. All successful, veteran craftspeople know that if they priced their craft using hourly wage as a criterion, they would be charging Macy's prices. People don't come to a craft show to pay such prices. Attempt to apply that formula and you will price yourself right out of business.

Quite naturally, you may ask, "Why can't I charge what I think I'm worth on an hourly basis?" Well, the answer is simple, if you can handle it. Essentially, in the craft world, the customer, far more than you, determines what your product is worth. We all have an inflated idea of the value of our work and time. It's human nature, particularly in the craft and art world.

When you work for an employer, he sets the hourly wage and if you don't believe it's sufficient recompense for your labor, you simply don't take the job, you quit, or maybe you go on strike. Now, of course, you can quit the crafts business, or not go into it in the first place, but the strike option is not available to you.

More to the point, you are now in the crafts business and have made a big investment. You're not likely to throw that out the window. Besides, you like the business. Unlike most jobs or professions, you are your own boss, you make your own hours, you go where you please, you set your own standards, you create what you want to create, and you move in a world in which you want to move. You probably don't want to give up all this freedom for a few extra dollars an hour.

Customer Reaction Can Help Determine Your Price

Since you cannot and should not attempt to explain to a customer why an item costs what it does or how many hours of labor you put in, the product must speak for you. Place too high a price tag on your craft, and the product's message to the customer is "too much." Conversely, price out of fear that you won't sell anything and the message to the customer is "too low." The customer becomes wary of the quality of your product and may not buy at all, or, will recognize a great bargain and buy you out. That can put you out of business too. I'll give you an example.

In 1982, when we designed our first picnic basket, we priced it at $28. We sold out at every show. We were as happy as the proverbial clams. We'd gross between $500 and $800 every show and thought we were doing great. The trouble was, I couldn't make baskets fast enough. It took the first year and advice from a veteran craftsperson to learn that those customers realized they were getting a tremendous bargain.

Eventually, we realized we were giving this basket away and, with much trepidation, raised the price to $40. Sales decreased! But, since our profit margin was higher, we made more money with less work. Then we got greedy and tried $50. Sales evaporated! We went back to $40, realizing that was the proper price at the time. Some sixteen years later, that basket still sold best at $48. Every time we raised it to $50, sales dropped. That fact involves another intriguing, mystifying, and often annoying pricing phenomenon with which you must learn to deal.

The Numbers Game of Pricing

There are in every business certain whole numbers that act like a wall or barrier beyond which the customer will not, for a given item, dip into her wallet or purse. Marketing and advertising people realized that years ago. You run into it every time you go to buy anything. Just remember how many products cost $4.95, $9.95, $19.95, $99.95, or $19,995.

I'm not suggesting that you use this technique. It is too much trouble in the crafts business. You don't have the time on a busy day to always be dealing with nickels and dimes. However, the idea points to the psychological phenomenon I mentioned.

Sometimes, just a dollar less will increase your sales, while a dollar more will reduce them. To give you a specific example: That first year in business, I had designed an odd-shaped fruit basket with a rope handle. It was very unusual, but it didn't sell. We carried fifteen of them with us to every show and every show we came home with fifteen. We priced them at $16 apiece. Exasperated, as I was tired of packing them in and out of the truck and having them take up valuable space on our shelf, I put a *sale* sign on them. We explained that we were no longer making that design and reduced the price to $15. We sold every basket that show. I, of course, then continued to produce that basket and $15 became the successful and appropriate price. Why $15 was right and $16 was too much, I'll never know. That is an intangible, even psychological phenomenon, involving every product in every marketplace.

Test Pricing

It was then that we learned that you must test price every piece of merchandise that you sell. This price testing is a never-ending process and you must be ready to make adjustments for the reasons already noted. Sometimes, in a really bad year, you may have to adjust downward in the middle of a season, sacrificing some profit as opposed to realizing no profit. But the longer you can keep your price structure steady, the better off you are.

Granting that testing your prices engages you in a nebulous, intangible, and often frustrating aspect of your operation, there are several ways to go about it. If you are producing a product that can generally be found at craft boutiques and other stores, one approach is to check the prices in those venues. You can count on the fact that the stores will have doubled the price on any item. It is necessary to their profit margin, since their operating expenses are much higher than yours. Therefore, you can probably assume that you can sell at half their price and be making a reasonable profit.

A second method of testing your prices is to evaluate the price your competition is asking. Since we already know, based on what we said earlier, that many craftspeople will be charging too much, if you think your version is as good or better than theirs, undersell them. This was something that we never had to do, as no one made a basket like ours. But, be warned: This may not make you popular with your competition, particularly if they follow the hourly wage approach, and they usually do.

During the hundreds of shows we did, we had many neighbors, at many shows, griping to us that they weren't selling because somebody else in the show was selling the same item "too low." Usually they would complain that the other guy "just had to be selling at a loss." The truth was that that was never the case. "The other guy" had simply found a way to produce the product for less and more efficiently, or perhaps his lifestyle required less profit, or perhaps he was simply not as greedy.

Whatever the reason, the craftsperson had no ethical right to complain. The crafts business is highly competitive, and such tactics are just a realistic part of the business. You are not in business to win popularity contests with your competitors. And you certainly are not going to go around discussing your prices with the competition, so you can agree on setting the same price. Do that and your competitor could be reaping real financial benefits while you lose money. You are in business to make the money you need to survive and profit. If you can satisfy your needs by underselling the competition, do it. You won't see the other guy that often anyway.

Once Again Variety

A third factor in pricing—and perhaps one of the most important—is to offer a wide variety of sizes and designs in all price ranges, but to make sure you can still produce a profit. This allows you to display a range of choices that can suit almost everyone's budget. Rhonda Blakely of Country Folk Art strongly urges craft artists to have a range of prices.

You will find this advice very helpful, especially when you are doing a show in an economically sluggish area or where economic forces have changed financial conditions. Our baskets ranged in price from $10 to $48. Therefore, we were able to retain our share of the market, no matter where we were and no matter what the economic situation. We didn't always make as much as we might have wanted, but who is always satisfied in life? Very often it was the smaller items that sold and kept us from losing money at a show.

Adjust Your Inventory

Think not only about how much inventory you should bring to a show, but also about what price range inventory you should carry with you. You may recall that I discouraged the idea of changing prices on a week-to-week basis and indicated that there were other ways to handle this problem. Here is one way:

Suppose you are scheduled for a show and you belatedly learn that there has been a downturn in the local economy. It is pointless to stock your booth with merchandise in your highest price range. As a matter of fact, no matter where we went, we never put more than one example of our highest-priced basket out front. People walk by, bend over, check the price tag, and walk on.

This is especially true in areas with a depressed economy. Don't even bring those high-priced items with you. Seeing the price will just discourage and often sadden potential customers. It reminds them of what they cannot afford. Better to have a fully stocked booth of items that are affordable to the people in the area, so everyone can feel they are getting a bargain. In the long run, you'll make more money and more friends.

The Special Order

Now a word about special ordering. It is inevitable and very probable that no matter how much inventory you have in your booth and how varied the selection open to the customer, a customer will be looking for something that you don't have. She may want a different color, a different size, a different something. That is a sale that is escaping you, unless you are prepared to take the order and ship it to the customer. Again, this is a subject that could have come under selling and marketing, because you should indicate to your customers that you are set up to meet a special-order demand. However, it is included in more detail here because it also involves pricing.

In some cases, if what the customer desires is not something that you have on the shelf, you may have the item at home. But, much more often than not, to provide the customer with what she is specifically ordering is going to cause you some inconvenience. You may have to go out and buy a special fabric or paint or wood or whatever. The customer may want a special design or size or any other number of possible changes. You can refuse and lose a customer or agree and establish a lasting relationship. We chose the latter, but, remember that you will probably be forced to consider some change of price.

When taking a special order, it is perfectly legitimate to inform the customer that you will have to charge more. Tell the customer the increased price and don't forget to inform her that the price includes not only the cost of shipping, but also of packaging for shipment. You should have these special-order prices ready and easily available for reference. If your merchandise is of varying size and weight, it will cost more or less to ship and will require more or less expensive packaging. Therefore, you should know the weight and size of every product you could be asked to ship, so that you can simply refer to a document on which you have the total cost already calculated and can quickly inform the customer of how much extra this service will cost. If she agrees, and she almost always will though it means a little extra work, it also means another sale now and often many sales in the future.

Early in our career, when Judy had to pack something for shipping, we ran around trying to find boxes at the supermarket, or wherever, trying to save money. We saved money, but lost time. We never had the right size box at the right time. We soon found that there are dozens of catalogues available that provide you with every conceivable means of shipping your merchandize in every size. From them, you can purchase boxes, bags, cellophane wrappings, labels, shipping tape, scales—just about anything you can think of relating to shipping a package.

Though out of business, we just received a catalogue of this type in the mail from Uline, a firm that operates out of Waukegan, Illinois. Uline has telephone, fax, and Internet capability to take your order. Another packaging-materials company specializing in bagging material and protective wrappings is North East Poly Bag, located in Sterling, Massachusetts. There are many more such manufacturers all over the country. However, if you cannot sustain this cost at the beginning, go to any flea market and you'll find someone selling plastic bags to use for packaging, or just hunt around the shopping mall, early in the morning, as we did, for empty cartons in which to ship your product. You can meet a lot of nice people at the rear of big stores, especially at Christmastime.

Another Reason to Review Your Pricing Structure

One last suggestion we would make regarding pricing has to do with record keeping, a task that can be very helpful in making price adjustments. Maintain a record of the price you place on every type of product you manufacture and review it on a quarterly basis. The purpose of this is twofold. It will provide you with a record of the number you have sold of each item in your inventory. More importantly, it will establish your leading sellers and what merchandise is selling poorly. If, based on your discussions with your customers, you are convinced that your pricing is affecting your sales, you can make the necessary price adjustments accordingly. Usually such adjustments are small, but they are very important to sales.

Cash Flow

Having read all these pricing techniques, perhaps you think we forgot that problem of hourly wages. We haven't, but we wanted to show you as many ways as possible to improve your sales and take your mind off that concept. However, if you insist on thinking in hourly terms, be reminded that the crafts business is about cash flow. It is a business that, when you are successful, will regularly put large amounts of money in your pocket. Your theoretical hourly wage is irrelevant. The hours you work will always be far more than you would at any nine-to-five job. But, so is the money you can make. We often made $5,000–$6,000 at many shows and many crafts merchants make a great deal more. If we worked an average of twelve hours a day, seven days a week, we were averaging almost sixty dollars an hour. Not many jobs pay that.

Realistically, if you are new to the business, you will probably not be making that kind of money until you perfect your manufacturing, selling, marketing, and pricing techniques, to mention only what has been discussed thus far. So, if you are dissatisfied with your profit margin, and expect to increase your profit (not your hourly wage), reevaluate your manufacturing techniques and cost of materials.

Ask yourself if you have done the necessary research to find new suppliers where you can purchase your materials for less money, but of equal quality. Can you find short cuts in the manufacturing process without sacrificing quality? Years into the business, we never ceased being surprised when we suddenly found an easier, less time-consuming way to do something, and would wonder, "Why didn't we think of that before?"

Concentrate on your successes and weed out the failures. Often enjoying what you're doing and the lifestyle you can now lead is the best reward.

ৡৰেই   েঠ৯   ৡৰেই

4

Strictly Business

"Being good in business is the most fascinating kind of art. . . . Making money is art and working is art and good business is the best art."
—ANDY WARHOL

NO DOUBT, ANDY WARHOL WAS CORRECT. JUDY IS AN artist at manipulating, keeping track of, and multiplying money. I've just wished that I could avoid writing this chapter, for if money management had been left to me, we never would have retired. While for some, managing money may be an "art," for most of us it is the most tedious and even threatening aspect of business. Too much creativity can lead not just to a lot of trouble with the IRS but, more important, to financial instability and even bankruptcy. Therefore, managing money may be the predominant reason why so many craftspeople fail to be successful. Creative and artistic people rarely think along the mechanical, logical, and practical lines necessary in a good accountant.

Finances boggle most of our brains. It takes a special kind of personality to be an accountant or tax consultant and to pore over figures day in and day out. Neither Judy nor I had the necessary credentials. One of us had to learn, however. Since, thank goodness, Judy was by far my superior in this area, she took on the tedious duty of record keeping. If you have a partner, and you cannot afford expert help, you should then make a decision in the early stages of developing your business about who will be the money manager. If you are a solo act, I'm afraid that you are probably stuck with the job. We will try to give you some general tips. This chapter, however, will not be devoted to a technical dissertation on bookkeeping, tax law, or other mathematical formulae. Neither Judy nor I are qualified to provide that kind of expertise.

Get Professional Help

If you hope to be successful in the craft world, no matter how talented you are or how beautiful your product, if you do not come to grips with the practical aspects of the crafts business, you will not be in business long. Our suggestion? If you can't or won't do your own accounting and bookkeeping, and if you can afford it, consult a professional as soon as you enter the crafts marketplace. If you are already in business and don't have a financial advisor, we strongly suggest that you find one. He will know what records your tax consultant will need. Most often, a financial consultant and tax consultant are the same person. Sit down with him and learn what you have to account for and what records you have to keep.

Once again, Judy and I learned the hard way. For the first few years, we were not aware of all the ramifications that could have saved us money. However, regardless of how good your tax consultant, there are certain general things you must do or you won't have any records to bring to him at the end of the year.

Open a Business Banking Account

Before you've invested, made, or spent a dime on your business, and after you've chosen a name for that business, go to your bank and open a separate business checking account in your business name. Thereafter, write checks relating to the business only out of this account. In your checkbook or on your computer, specify what kind of bill you are paying, such as: shop supplies, show fees, postage, advertising, office supplies, legal fees, and the like. This is essential to keeping an accurate account of your financial transactions and cannot be emphasized enough. Any large purchases, such as your computer, production machinery, or business vehicles, may be depreciated or used as deductions. Your accountant is the best one to advise you regarding this aspect of your accounting.

Keeping an accurate business account is absolutely essential when you sit down with your tax consultant to explain your expenses. He will always want those expenses broken down for IRS purposes. By breaking your expenses into categories (such as telephone, electronic, travel, cost of goods sold, etc.), you also create a helpful tool to evaluate how your business spends money. This should enable you to budget and, in many cases, cut back on expenses.

These expenses are enumerated on Schedule C of your tax form. It is best to consult a professional in advance to verify all expenses that you may legally take. Then, when you write checks to pay your business bills, identify to which of these categories they were applied. Doing this not only saves time when tax deadlines roll around, but it enables you to better judge just what your product is costing and hence assists you in setting the most appropriate and fair price. That is, *fair* to both you and your customers.

An excellent discussion of income taxes can be found in *Legal Guide for the Visual Artist* by Tad Crawford, an attorney who represented many artists and artists' groups before becoming the publisher of Allworth Press (and this book).

Avoid Commingling Funds

Maintained both for legal and tax reasons, meticulous records are a must. You should always avoid commingling your business funds with money used to manage home expenses, food, rent/mortgage, entertainment, and the like. Commingling funds will make it impossible for you to know—and positively establish on your tax return—what money went into and out of the business and what did not. Never use your business account for any purpose other than your business or you will find your business and private financial dealings hopelessly confused. You will never know how much profit you are making or how much loss you are suffering.

Small Business Regulations, Resale Permits, and Licenses

Research your state's regulations on small businesses. You will probably need a resale permit or business license, as you will have to pay state sales tax on a yearly, biannual, or quarterly basis. In California, we had to pay sales tax quarterly; here this is determined by the State Board of Equalization. So as not to be caught financially unprepared, we recommend that you set aside the amount of money that you owe the government after each show; those monies might even be placed in a separate checking account earmarked for taxes and used only to make such payments. That way you will not be scrounging for money or depending on the next show to make a payment from the last show. That applies not only to money that you will eventually have to pay the federal and state governments in the form of income taxes, but also money you owe in the form of sales tax.

In some cases, as in California, where we primarily did business, you may start out paying sales tax annually and then, as we were, be moved by the state to quarterly payments. Remember that sales tax is different from county to county and state to state. In some places you will pay city sales tax as well as state tax. So, depending on where you are doing business, you must know the tax laws and tax rates in that community.

As an example, in Nevada, the sales tax is paid only to the state of Nevada. But since the Nevada tax collectors do not want to wait until the end of the year for nonresidents to pay that tax or have to keep records of everyone who owes Nevada money, sales tax is collected at the end of each show by the promoter. When we did shows in Nevada, each craftsperson signed a slip indicating his gross income at the show and then enclosed in an envelope the amount of money or percentage of that gross that the state required for sales tax. The promoter then was responsible for submitting the total amount to the state.

Such tax is also subject to change from year to year, usually on the upward side, so you must remember to obtain a chart from the promoter of the show each time you are in a new city, county, parish, or state. The chart will give you the exact percentage you need to pay, wherever you are. In California, the State Board of Equalization, from whom we received our resale permit and to whom we paid our sales tax, also provided us with such a chart. We carried it to every show, sometimes providing the information to other craftspeople and even the promoter. You will have to check these regulations in your state to assess and add to the price of every item you sell.

Assessing Sales Tax to the Customer

Basically, there are two ways to impose sales tax: You can roughly include the sales tax in the total price you are charging for your product or you can apply the necessary tax to the price you put on your product, at the time you ring up the purchase. We highly recommend the second option, and some states require it.

If you choose the first option and include the tax in the total price, you will be changing your price tags at every show that takes place in a county, city, or state that requires a different percentage than the last place in which you did a show. Very few locales impose the same sales tax, and because there are different regulations all over the United States, there is no way to provide you with general guidelines. Besides, the information usually changes from year to year.

As well, including the tax in the total price requires that you hang a sign informing the customers that your price includes sales tax. Psychologically, when people are comparison shopping, that addition to the total price may make a significant difference to many would-be customers—to your detriment. You are presenting your product as even more expensive, sometimes too expensive, as compared to your competition. Eight percent added to a $50 purchase is $4 more. Human nature being what it is, those few dollars more may hinder your sales, even though people are paying the same total amount when they complete the transaction at your cash register.

The reason for the different reaction at the register is that once a customer is at the counter and ready to pay for something she has chosen, she rarely rebels against the tax or decides not to buy because of it. She is accustomed to paying tax for everything she purchases anywhere, so she doesn't notice the difference between your asking price on the price tag and the purchase price at the counter. Besides, once she has the product in hand, having decided that she wants it, she is psychologically committed to the purchase and less likely to change her mind about buying it.

The Resale Permit

Having often referred to the resale permit, I should mention that it may or may not be required in your state. When such a permit is required, as in California, it is very important to you. Carry it with you whenever you are purchasing materials for your business. Most suppliers will defer sales tax if you have such a permit. The resale permit works in the following way:

If any of the materials that you purchase from a supplier are either items to be resold after some decorative embellishing by you, or are materials used to manufacture your product, the resale permit entitles the purchaser to not collect sales tax on those items. That is why it has the name—*resale permit*—and why you carry it with you at all times. The merchant selling you your materials will need to see the permit and will fill out a form with your permit number on it. You will sign this form and the merchant will then sell you the material without charging you the sales tax. This is because the item or material is going to be "resold" at a later date, at which time sales tax is added by you to the purchase price of your merchandise. You as the seller are then merely forwarding the required amount to the necessary agency, city, county, state. Remember that it is then actually the customer who is paying the tax. You are only collecting it for the agency. Whether such resale permits are required or optional in your state or are referred to by a different name is something that you need to research. It's worth your time to do so.

In our case, such materials as lumber, fabric, paint, stain, glue, and the like—all the materials that became part of our product—were subject to this sales-tax exemption. Later, as baskets, the finished product was "resold," and the sales tax was collected at that time. As a manufacturer, this exemption may allow you to lower the price you put on your merchandise.

Since you deferred the sales tax until the time of sale, your product cost less to produce, thus benefiting both the consumer and you. The total cost of all that sales tax on material, if purchased and paid for by you without a resale license, would add a great deal more to the price of your product, and you would necessarily have to charge the customer more. Since you can sell it now for less, that makes your product that much more attractive, especially if competitors are not using this method and are therefore setting higher prices. Judy and I cannot stress enough that attention to these kinds of financial details is essential if you are to be competitive and successful in the craft world.

Your Suppliers and Your Accounts

Line up your suppliers and establish accounts with them under your business name. With most suppliers, you can work out a standard discount based on how much you expect to spend in their store. This is a discount separate from the sales-tax benefit mentioned above. Inform your suppliers that part or most of your purchases will be with a resale permit. You can set up the account so that your purchases are divided into "costs of goods sold" and other general shop or production supplies.

If you are just starting out in the business, you may not be able to establish the arrangements specified above immediately. If your credit rating is good and you can establish a dependable financial track record with your suppliers, receiving a discount should be easy. They need only see that you are spending a great deal of money in their business establishment and paying your monthly bill regularly. When the lumber company near us realized that we would be spending $500–$1,000 a month in their lumberyard, they quickly gave us a 10 percent discount rather than see us go up the road and buy our lumber elsewhere. Depending on your age, you might also find that the store grants a senior citizen discount that can further reduce your costs.

While you are establishing these accounts, check every resource for your supplies. This applies to veterans in the business as well as newcomers. Maybe even more so to veterans, for once accounts are established for a few years, your busy schedule and the convenience of the accounts you already have tend to cause you to forget or get lazy about looking for new suppliers.

New competition is always out there and may give you a better deal. Most often, there are many companies making the same product at different prices, or there are discount dealers who supply on a broad national or even international level in such volume that the cost can be as much as 50 percent less than your neighborhood store. If one supplier won't accommodate you, another will.

Catalogue Suppliers

With our busy schedule, whenever possible, we found it much easier to order our supplies by phone and have them shipped directly to our doorstep. Saving such time and energy assists in manufacturing and also saves money, thereby increasing profits.

Many companies sell fabrics, wood—every conceivable material you may need—and most provide catalogues describing their product line. One company mailed us swatches of fabric on a regular basis as samples from which we could select and order. We ordered bolts of fabric, and when we ordered by phone, if the material was in stock, the bolts of fabric were usually on our doorstep within a week.

Of course, when you start out, you may not want to order in such large quantities, but as you become increasingly successful and develop confidence in your product, the larger the quantity of material you buy, the less expensive it is. Hence, ordering in bulk is cost-effective and time-efficient. It will help you to keep your prices down and still maintain quality and profit.

Once your accounts are established, be sure to pay all your bills out of your business account. If you run out of money, transfer funds from your personal to your business account, but make sure you keep a record of the transfer. Later, when you start making money, pay back the personal account. Always deposit money made from your crafts business into your business account. If, due to some circumstance, you need to withdraw money from your business account for some personal use, remember to always make a note of the transfer and the reason for it. And pay it back! You may in fact want to pay yourself a salary and write yourself a check, just as you may do for anyone working for you. That will depend on your cash flow in the beginning.

Keeping Your Records

It is essential that you keep comprehensive and accurate records of all transactions relating to your business. Getting yourself organized in every aspect of your business is vital to your success, but nowhere more essential than in this area. Therefore, we suggest that you establish a filing system separate from any other personal account records you may keep. If you don't have a computer, you may simply buy a standard and traditional accounting records book at any stationery store. If you have never used such a book, you might want to take a basic course in accounting at a local community college, or buy one of the many textbooks on the market.

If you already have a computer and you are comfortable using it, you may prefer to set up any one of a number of programs designed for business accounting. The nice part of such programs is that they will do all of the figuring for you. You just have to plug in the numbers. If you keep records after every show, as you should, you will have a running record of exactly where you stand financially in relation to your business at any given moment you need the information. Into the computer go all your expenses for postage, legal and consultant fees, gasoline and oil, vehicle repairs, advertising, food and lodging costs, equipment purchases—everything relating to the business.

When you are selling at a craft show, make sure to give every customer a receipt for her purchase and keep a copy for your records. That way, you will have a running account of every transaction in which you have engaged and know exactly what profit (hopefully) you are making or how much money you are losing. Make sure you keep the actual receipts and other paperwork, long after you have filed your tax returns. Should you ever be audited (a hideous experience), the IRS agent will want to see them.

While on the subject of what records to keep, we suggest that you keep your inventory records of production broken down by month. In other words, keep a record of just how many of each item you made each month. We discovered the advantage of this by happenstance early in our career. Keeping track of this information enabled us to review those records the following year, compare them with our sales record for the same months the previous year, when doing essentially the same shows, and have a pretty good approximation of just how much material we had to buy and how much of the finished product we had to manufacture for a given show and even for the entire new season.

As we got older and our bodies were wearing out, I must admit that we hated reviewing and maintaining this list, as we dreaded knowing that we had to look forward to manufacturing some 4,000–5,000 baskets. But we did it, because it was useful and necessary. I told you it isn't all fun—it's about money.

As part of your record keeping, know how much of a product you have made to date, week to week. As the year progresses, you will know how many of that item you have sold, and when, and where you sold it. This will also tell you immediately which items are selling well and which are selling poorly or not at all, as compared to the previous year. You don't want to waste money on materials or waste effort producing losing items.

If you wish to deduct the business use of your home for tax purposes, talk to your tax consultant to make sure that your business qualifies for the deduction and how you go about keeping the records necessary to take the deduction. With all this information plugged into your computer, you simply have to print it out at the end of the year and take it to your tax consultant. We should add that, if you are personally knowledgeable and proficient in doing your own taxes, certainly do so, since it saves you money. Judy chose to do it for us because, early on, she had learned the essentials and, later, with all the records at hand in the computer, she only had to fill out the forms. We also have a son-in-law who is a CPA. On the other hand, it still is time-consuming—time you could be devoting to your product and being creative, or getting a much needed rest. Your choice!

Business-Related Use of Your Vehicle

In order for use of your vehicle to be deducted on Schedule C of your income tax return, you have to keep good mileage records on every business-related trip; that is, to and from shows, buying trips for supplies, even going to the post office to ship an order. Another approach is to use a standard mileage deduction specified by the IRS, but it won't add up to nearly as much as if you keep your own records.

Judy and I developed the practice of keeping a book in the glove compartment of our vehicle specifically to keep those records, using the odometer to give us exact mileage readings. We also kept a folder in the truck in which we placed all documents relating to repair, maintenance, gas and oil expenditures, and the receipts for money spent in this way. If you follow our example, you will have accurate records and at the end of the year, you can simply note the total miles the vehicle was driven, and subtract the total number of miles that were business related. If that figure is at least 50 percent of the total miles driven, you can take the business deduction for your vehicle. We would then just plug those figures into the proper place in our computer business program.

All of this advice relating to your vehicle is really very simple and made even simpler if you always use the same vehicle. Record keeping is less likely to become confused. We virtually never used the truck for anything else—a good idea anyway, as it saves wear and tear on the vehicle that is essential to your business.

Oh! You should also remember and record your vehicle's registration fee and your insurance costs. Please keep in mind, though, that tax codes change yearly, so even the most minor advice we suggest here is subject to change. Tax requirements that were applicable a few years ago may no longer be applicable. Be sure to talk to your accountant for specific, up-to-date details.

Establish a Mailing List

By taking contact information from checks or customers' IDs, you can, with the customers' permission, establish a mailing list. We would suggest doing this, starting at your very first show. If you don't do it, you're missing a great sales opportunity. A simple way to begin such a list is to hang up or display on a table a clipboard with name and address forms. We suggest you do not refer to it as a "mailing list," since people don't want a lot of junk mail. Just tell the customers that if they fill it out, you'll mail them your show schedule next year.

If a customer pays by check, take her name and address from the check before you deposit it. Should the customer use a credit card, have preprinted index cards available on which she can provide you with mailing information. Or if the customer pays cash, ask her for her address, explaining that you intend to mail her a yearly notice of your craft show schedule. If she does not wish to give her address to you (perhaps she considers it an invasion of privacy or does not desire more "junk mail"), politely accept her reason.

Over the years, this list will grow quite large. At today's postage rates, this can be expensive, particularly since a certain percentage will be returned as "No longer at this address." This does add up and can seem like a waste of money, time, and effort. However, it is a legitimate business expense for tax purposes and well worth the hours, the labor, and the expense. Also, these days you may be able to build an e-mail list in addition to a snail-mail list. Doing this can put a lot of dollars in your pocket instead of Uncle Sam's because of the savings on postage.

Of course, you don't want to spend any more money than necessary, so to minimize your snail-mail cost you may choose to devise some personal method of paring down the list. Based on thirty-two years of experience, Jim and Fran Seeley recommend winnowing your mailing list every three years. Depending on the size of the mailing list, you may also want to purchase any one of a number of good mailing-list computer programs that print out addressed labels, once you input the data. This is a big time and effort saver, as opposed to writing out envelopes or postcards by hand.

As to those returned as "No longer at this address," just erase the name from your list and accept those that are returned as part of the cost of doing business. After your first year in business, notifying customers from the previous year that you will be in their town again and providing them with your entire schedule for the year is well worth the cost. It is also a deductible business expense, as are the computer programs. If you are dubious about this form of advertising and business expense, we can assure you that we found that, even if a customer doesn't make a purchase at your booth, she often comes by to thank you for notifying her that the show is taking place. As with any of us on a hectic schedule, she may not have known about the craft show, forgotten the date, or forgotten the show altogether. She'll tell you that she didn't want to miss the show and appreciates your kindness in mailing her a notification. This pays dividends in your customer relations. She will be back when she wants what you have to sell.

Jim and Fran ran the statistics on their use of a mailing list, having kept accurate records of repeat customers who purchased from them as a result of mailed notification. They found that customers they had personally invited to a show accounted for 40 to 45 percent of their sales, and these sales, because these customers spent more than their uninvited customers, accounted for 60 percent of their gross sales.

Providing your customers with your schedule is good public relations and good advertising, regardless of whether or not they make a purchase from you. From the advertising perspective, you've reminded them of you, your product, and your business. If they don't buy today, they'll often buy another day, as long as you have a good product.

It takes a few years to develop a substantial list. Naturally, you only mail notices to people who live within the general area of the show and are likely to attend. Judy and I never did a statistical breakdown, but Jim and Fran did and computed that if you spend $1,000 on mailing and gross $50,000 that year, it translates to spending two cents to generate each dollar. We had a smaller mailing list and found that profit earned from purchases made by about ten customers to whom we mailed show notification, paid for all our mailing expense; everybody else was a bonus. If you use your computer to accomplish this task, it is, over time, much cheaper than ordering at a print shop and less time consuming than mailing by hand.

In the final analysis, this whole process is just another important form of promoting yourself and your product for which Jim and Fran gave me a little jingle: Early to bed, early to rise, Work like hell and advertise.

Buy a Cash Register

Before you do your first show, go to any business supply store and purchase a cash register. Buy a register that supplies duplicate receipts and that is powered by battery or will plug into a standard wall outlet. Such registers come equipped with rechargeable batteries and are essential at outdoor shows, where there is never an available source of electricity. Sometimes, when we're indoors, the power may go out; then our register automatically switches over to battery power.

Using a cash register is the most professional way to do business, and that's the image you want to create. It is also the most secure. Working out of a tin box looks amateurish and gives the customer the impression that you are nonprofessional. The tin box also makes for unreliable record keeping, often prompting you to commingle funds. At lunchtime, you are hungry, so you grab money from the box and run off to eat. Later in the afternoon, you leave your partner in the booth, remove some money from the box (you don't even count it to see how much), and run off to buy some supplies or make a purchase at another craft booth. By the end of the weekend you have no idea how much money you have spent in this careless way.

The cash register gives you a continuing record of your sales transactions. You will know exactly how many sales you made and for how much money. When you cash out your register at the end of the day, if your cash is less than your receipts, you know how much of your profit you already spent.

Not only will most good registers give you a total of the amount you earned that day when you cash out, but they can also be programmed to break down your sales receipts so you know your net sales, sales tax, and gross totals. This gives you the exact amount you should set aside to pay your sales tax.

Most important, your money is safer in a locked cash register drawer. There are times when you will just have to leave the booth unattended and, unless it is going to be for an extended period of time, you don't want to have to take all of your cash from the tin box or walk around everywhere with a tin box in your hand. A register that can be secured to your countertop is the most preferable. Let's face it, all kinds of people come to a craft show—particularly street fairs and festivals in the park where the beer and wine flows freely. I don't know how many craftspeople we met over the years who left their booth and returned to find that their cash box was gone.

This brings us to a final few words about the cash register. Remember to bring cash and change to put in the register at the start of the working day. More than once we forgot and one of us had to leave the show and go to the bank to withdraw operating money, especially change. Having to do this is very inconvenient and in some cases, impossible, if there is no bank or ATM in the near vicinity. Once we actually were forced to borrow operating capital, which is amateurish and embarrassing. Furthermore, bring a few hundred dollars. People seem to bring big bills to craft shows and it is not unusual for your first customer of the day to purchase a $10 item and hand you a $100 bill. By the end of a good selling day, your register will most often be jammed with big bills, while you will usually be hard-pressed for singles and change.

Design Patents, Copyrights, and Trademarks

If you have created a new product and are concerned that someone may copy and sell your idea, it is possible to obtain what is known as a design patent on your product. This is, however, a complicated legal procedure. There are attorneys out there who specialize in patent law and nothing else. We will make no attempt here to discuss it in any detail. It is possible to research it yourself at any library. You might wish to buy or refer to a copy of *The Patent Guide,* by Carl Battle (Allworth Press), who is an attorney specializing in the subject of patents. But, we would recommend that you take no action in this regard without legal advice.

We had one occasion when we found it necessary to seek the legal advice of a patent attorney. It involved a craftsperson based in another state, but selling at shows in our state. She claimed that we stole her design for a paper-plate holder, stating that her design was patented. The truth is we had never seen her work, but we went to an attorney for advice. Some $500 later, he had looked up her design and there was absolutely no resemblance between her product and ours, other than that they were both paper-plate holders. He wrote a letter with a picture of our paper-plate holder to her attorney, pointing out the many differences in design and material, and that was the end of the matter.

Obviously, it is a very expensive process and, frankly, for most products, rarely worthwhile. It is too easy for artisans to make enough variations in a product design they have stolen to make it legal. Lawyers will gain a lot more than you will. They make at least $100 an hour, and usually much more.

One technique that some craftspeople use to protect the design of their product is to mail themselves a certified letter marked "return receipt requested," describing the product and enclosing a picture of it. The letter may also include a description of how the product is produced and what materials are used. However, this "poor man's copyright" approach has no legal status and we strongly advise against relying on it. If your product is worth protecting, consult a lawyer so you can do it properly.

The question of whether or not your particular craft qualifies to be copyrighted is another complicated legal question that we cannot and should not go into here. Generally speaking, pictorial, graphic, and sculptural works are copyrightable. A definition given by Tad Crawford in *The Legal Guide for the Visual Artist,* which thoroughly covers copyright, is that "work must be original and creative." Clearly, this is a pretty broad definition and is actually far more specifically defined in the book. Audiovisual works represent another category of art that can be copyrighted. Therefore, some artisans will produce work that can be protected through the use of the copyright and others will find that their work cannot be so protected. We can only refer you to the above-titled book, which also lists where you may seek the advice of specialists in this field of law. You may choose to go to the public library and do your own research, but be aware that the once simple, common-law copyright was virtually eliminated in 1978. Copyright is now statutory and far more complicated. You should consult experts, for only they can tell you whether your craft can be copyrighted and what benefit that would be to you.

In the second chapter of this book, we addressed the importance of the business name as a sales and promotional tool. Trademarks are names or logos that identify a particular business as the source of goods marked with that name or logo. A great book on this protection is *The Trademark Guide* by Lee Wilson (Allworth Press). If the public is going to know that goods with a certain name or logo come from your company, consider getting a lawyer's help in filing your trademark (but keep in mind you may have protection even if you didn't file).

A Crucial Related Problem

The subject that is discussed next could be included in chapter 7, "Booth Setup and Booth Display," because it will be when your booth is fully set up, your crafts on display, and you are engaged in selling your craft that you will be confronted with *this* problem. However, the subject is included in this chapter in that it specifically relates to design patents and protecting your product.

Sometimes you will notice a typical tourist type who is just taking a picture of his or her wife or husband standing in front of your booth. Or tourists will take a picture inside the booth as a record of their having been there and attended the show. This happened to us a lot at Lake Tahoe, where there are thousands of tourists from all over the world and the lake is a beautiful, scenic background. They would even take photos holding baskets in their hands that they had purchased from us, and ask us to pose in the pictures. This is fine, no problem, and you should always accommodate your customers, if possible, when they compliment you by making such a request after a purchase.

The serious and difficult problem with which you will occasionally have to deal involves the person who walks into your booth with a sketch pad and starts drawing your designs or the person with a camera who stands outside, or even inside the booth, and starts to photograph every item. Because you are busy or the booth and aisles are crowded, you may not even realize that it is happening until it is too late. When that happens, there is nothing you can do about it except to talk to the person, ask him to stop taking pictures or sketching your product. This person is not a tourist; this person is a thief.

In some cases, people merely want to copy your design in order to go home and make the product themselves for their own use. There really is no harm in this; after all, they could buy your product, take it home, and do the same thing. There is really nothing you can do about that.

The serious problem and threat to your business is the people who intend to produce the product themselves and sell it (who knows where). They will certainly be in competition with you and will be using your creation. Such a person may be an agent for a manufacturing concern, most often overseas or across the border. The intent is to reproduce your product, taking advantage of the much cheaper cost of labor out of this country, and then ship it back to the United States and sell it here, undercutting your price.

If such people are inside your booth, you have every right to ask them to stop drawing or photographing. If these people refused, either Judy or I would then position ourselves in front of them, blocking their line of sight to whatever they were copying on paper or attempting to photograph. Most of the time, this prompted them to leave the booth, particularly if we told them (whether it was true or not) that we had design patents on our work and that if they reproduced anything we created, we would sue them.

In this regard, you may, unfortunately, have a few obstinate types who refuse to stop either drawing or taking pictures. They will usually assert that "This is a free country and that they can take pictures anywhere they want." This is true, only to a certain extent. You do not have control of the aisles, especially at shows to which people paid admission. If they stand in the aisle or street, all you can do is be equally obnoxious and continue to block their view. We only had to resort to this technique twice. It takes a lot of self-control to deal with this problem, so be ready to adopt the necessary attitude.

As a merchant, however, you *do* have control of your booth space, as you have leased it for the time of the show. So, in both instances, in a polite manner and attempting to avoid an obnoxious incident, explain your rights, ask the person to leave and if he doesn't, then do what you first politely threaten—call the promoter. The promoter or security personnel will take charge of the matter at any good show, sometimes escorting the interlopers off the premises. Many of the bigger indoor promotions don't allow cameras into the building in order to protect the craftspeople from this kind of intrusion. For this reason, I had to obtain permission from the promoter to take the indoor photographs you see in this book. I also obtained signed permission forms from every craftsperson whose booth display Judy photographed. Even for this book, some artisans refused, quite naturally afraid that their design or idea could be stolen by someone reading the book.

Small Business Insurance

As you travel from show to show, you are going to be faced with certain risk factors at those that serve beer or wine. Under these conditions, you may encounter annoying and disreputable members of the public or, sometimes, perfectly well-behaved people, either of whom may have some sort of accident in your booth. They may be drunk and disorderly and in this condition do damage to your booth, merchandise, or both. They might simply trip on the carpeting or some object in your booth space. Perhaps, in crowded, cramped conditions they are jostled, stumble, and fall. No matter how it happens, the individual could decide to sue you and your business for damages, should she sustain any injury.

During the years we were in business, we never covered ourselves with any form of liability insurance. Were we beginning our career in this far more litigious age, we might well do so and we recommend that you investigate the cost of this coverage. A number of insurance companies will give you ratings. The cost will depend on whether you want only liability insurance covering injury to people who are in your booth or you wish to also cover damage to you and your merchandise. Had we chosen to take out such insurance, it would have been liability only, as it would not have been financially worthwhile to cover our merchandise. The likelihood of the entire booth burning down or being swept away in a flood was pretty remote. Nor was it worthwhile to try to cover ourselves for the theft of a few baskets or some minor damage. Therefore, no attempt is made here to estimate costs to you for such insurance. How much your policy will cost, if you can find the appropriate insurance company that underwrites such liability, involves too many variables and is particularly dependent on the estimated value of the merchandise you take to a show and how high a coverage you decide to select. Remember, insurance is to protect against big losses that you can't pay out of your own pocket. If you do get coverage, consider lowering your premium by having a high deductible (the amount you have to pay before the insurance kicks in)—as long as you can afford to pay the deductible amount.

Merchant Charge Accounts

Establishing merchant charge capabilities with a local bank that includes the use of a credit card charge machine is now a must in the crafts business. A merchant networking service will program the machine and you will then need to contact the individual credit card companies—Visa, Amex, MasterCard,

Discover, and so on—to establish your accounts. You are then linked through the service directly into your business bank account. It's possible that you may have some difficulty finding a bank, because some won't set up such accounts unless you have a storefront. But more banks are now providing for the establishment of accounts that use a card-swipe machine as the demand for the service has increased dramatically since we first entered the crafts business.

Purchase of these machines and the accompanying cellular phone and service used to be expensive—as much as a $1,000 to purchase the machine when we bought one. Nowadays, it is much more likely that the machine will be lent or leased to you, for a nominal fee, by the vendor for the duration of your service contract. Therefore, the machine ultimately costs you virtually nothing and whatever costs you do incur are, or at least have traditionally been, tax-deductible business expenses.

Under any circumstances, the cost of doing business with the card swipe machine is more than worth the initial expense and the 2–5 percent of each transaction taken by the credit card company (the exact percentage depends on the volume of business and the terms of your deal). We found that our sales and, hence, our profits, rose by 33 percent after we obtained the capability to accept charge cards. Like it or not, our nation's economy runs on credit and, as a businessperson, you'll need to recognize and take advantage of this economic reality. If you don't, you will lose many customers to some competitor who possesses charge capability. Charge capability offers your crafts business numerous other advantages. Each credit card with which you contract will provide you with signs that are used to display what credit cards you accept. You should hang your signs at the front of and inside your booth, so that every customer is aware in advance that you accept charge cards. You will find that many craftspeople accept only cash and checks and some will not even take a check. They are sadly limiting their moneymaking ability: The fact that you do adds to yours.

Another advantage to you when you accept credit cards is that, unlike a check, you will know immediately if the customer's account is solvent. A printout in the window of the machine gives you that information. Naturally, this is very embarrassing to most customers as they fumble for an explanation, but rarely do you lose a sale. Usually, the customer just pulls out another credit card from her purse or wallet or she pays cash.

Relative to record keeping, it is extremely important that you retain and file all your records of transactions made over the machine and that you do so faithfully, not only for tax purposes and for your personal accounting system. On some occasions, you may receive a notice in the mail of a charge back. All too frequently, you have to respond immediately or lose the amount of money the sale represented. Developing a quick, easy filing system in this regard is a must. The reasons for a charge back are many, but most often it comes as a result of a customer simply forgetting that she made the purchase. Most crafts businesses have unusual names that give the customer no hint as to what the purchase might have been. She has made purchases in a number of craft booths, at a number of shows, and has simply forgotten the purchase she made in your booth. The card may have been used by the husband, to buy a surprise present and so the wife, unaware of the purchase, challenges the charge on her statement.

In this case, you will receive notice from the bank that a customer has challenged a charge on her statement. You then have to quickly call the bank to show proof of sale. Your proof is your copy of the signed receipt the machine produced. You must keep all these receipts in order and readily accessible, so you can expeditiously respond to the problem. Be very conscientious in this regard: If you can't prove that the customer made the purchase, you will be required to refund that amount to the bank, which will, in essence, have made a gift of your merchandise to some customer.

Accepting Checks

Many, many craftspeople are afraid to and often refuse to accept a customer's personal check, and so lose the customer. There is no greater bonehead approach to business. In seventeen years, some five hundred shows, and who knows how many thousands of checks, we had no more than fifteen checks bounce and only four that went uncollected.

Customers at a craft show are honest people. They don't come to a craft show to rip the merchants off. We found that when a check did bounce, it was most often because some husband forgot to deposit his paycheck or it was due to a simple, mathematical mistake, the kind we have all made at one time or another. Refuse to accept them and you will be giving away far more profit than you could possibly lose if a check does bounce. You will just be sending your business to a competitor, losing not just that sale, but any repeat business that customer might have given you.

Your Business Work Routine

Because it isn't fun and it's hardly creative, it is very easy to procrastinate about developing a business-related schedule, similar to your craft-producing schedule. Judy and I strongly recommend that it is best to quickly learn to make it part of your regular work routine.

Judy always did her accounting and bookkeeping on Monday morning, the day after a show. First, she did all the accounting work while all the information was fresh in her memory. Then she immediately went to the bank and deposited all the money. Usually, she completed all the business-related activity by noon and she could return to the creative work and concentrate on making baskets.

Granted, this part of the business is tedious and, for most people, not particularly enjoyable, but it is actually the most important aspect of your craft work because it represents your bottom line—money. You will lose a lot of it and never know where it went if you don't apply yourself conscientiously to this vital area of the business. As you become a regular participant in the crafts business, and each week you meet and observe many fellow artisans, you will instinctively know, just by looking at their operations, which ones treat this aspect of the business seriously and professionally and which do not. Imitate those who do, engage them in friendly conversation, and learn the tricks of the trade. We are sure that you will find that, invariably, those craftspeople who appear the most professional are the most successful, because they operate according to the same basic principles that we advise.

The Need for Record Keeping

Failure to keep accurate records and attend to them regularly and efficiently may mean not only wasted time later in the year when you try to catch up, but also the loss of considerable income. At year's end, when tax time rolls around, you don't want to be hunting for receipts you didn't save, trying to remember how many times you drove to town for supplies, or rummaging through a carton full of slips of paper just to answer your tax consultant's questions. Under the existing pressures we are describing, you will not be able to remember all the details of the preceding year, and you will have lost much of the corroborating evidence of the claims you wish to make on your tax form.

In every small business, the owner wears a number of hats. The difference between small business and big business is that big business hires people to wear each separate hat. As a craftsperson and a small businessperson, you must wear virtually every hat most of the time—and more than one at the same time—until you are well established and making a very good income. The reality is that you just can't afford to do it any other way, especially in the early years that you are in business.

As time goes by and you can afford it, decide what parts of the manufacturing process you enjoy and take the least of your time. Then decide what operation is most time-consuming and laborious. No matter how creative a person you may be, when you are manufacturing a product repetitiously, it will become boring. Certain aspects of the process will always remain a challenge, while others you will dread. That is the time to hire someone to do the bookkeeping or bulk sewing or whatever part of the entire manufacturing process is the most tedious for you.

Because the crafts business is labor-intensive and cannot, as we said before, be evaluated on an hourly basis, your cash flow provides the necessary financial leverage. If you've run your business correctly, you'll have the money to pay for extra help. You will then find that hiring someone to handle a specific aspect of your business enables you to generate greater profit, in spite of the cost. Your time and energy then can be better spent on creating a better product. You will also relieve some of the tensions and pressure that can be so frustrating and debilitating; as a result, you'll have more fun.

5

Selecting Your Shows

NOW YOU ARE READY TO GO INTO BUSINESS AND SELL your product. You've worked hard and produced what you believe to be a sufficient amount of inventory. Your product is as beautiful as you know how to make it, the quality as good as money can buy. You haven't skimped on any of the materials in your product and you believe you are asking a fair price and can expect to make a fair profit. Now for the $64,000 question: Where do you sell it? How do you find the places where your product will be most marketable, where it will be most in demand? Where do you find that buying public anxious to make you rich?

How *Not* to Pick Your Shows

Before we tell you what positive steps to take to find your market, we think it's crucial to explain to you first what *not* to do. Ordinarily, when instructing anyone on any subject, using the positive side of the teaching coin is preferable. But in the matter of selecting craft shows, we must show the negative examples first, to help you proceed with the necessary caution.

The reality of the ever-growing crafts business is that there are just too many shows out there every weekend—too many potentially costly mistakes—should you select the wrong shows. Particularly in the beginning, it is much easier to work by a process of elimination, scratching all the undesirable shows. Otherwise, you will find yourself at some, maybe too many, of those very shows. So, while no one can predict exactly where your market *isn't*, using this approach, with some important tips, we can help you find where your best markets *are*.

As in every other aspect of the crafts business, Judy and I had little guidance our first year in business. We had never heard of or seen a *Crafts Fair Guide* and so we chose our first shows essentially through word of mouth or because we saw a show being advertised on a poster. We were such rank beginners that, until we (quickly) learned better, sometimes we would just drive up to a show with our truck full of inventory, expecting that all we had to do was to show up, unload, set up, and sell.

A few times that approach was actually successful, because the promoter received a number of cancellations and no-shows. It was, as a matter of fact, one of those small promoters who explained to us that normally we had to apply in advance and gave us applications for his future shows. As a result, for most of our first year in business, we were doing nothing but little, small-town street fairs, twenty-five booths in a show, the town so out of the way that the only customers were the residents—all 250 of them.

What would happen at these shows was that Harriet, in the booth next to us, would tell us about a particular show for which she was booked two weeks later and she would expound the virtues of the show, claiming that last year it was a "great show." Two weeks later we would end up in another nearby, small-town community and there would be Harriet, waving and smiling brightly, but nary a customer when the show opened.

Another time it was Joe, happily selling his little wooden toys, who told us that a show he was doing the following week had always been a "great show"— for the last six years. Then Edna informed us that a certain show was a surefire winner and we shouldn't miss it. "The people will love your stuff," she would rave. And so on and so forth.

We took everybody's tips and recommendations, believed their every word, and innocently applied to enter, and when we were accepted, packed ourselves off to these shows—only to come home, if we were lucky, with $300–$400 in our pocket. One time, our total take was $35. The only saving grace was that most of these shows were close enough that we could drive home each night and save ourselves motel and food expenses. That was all that was keeping us from plunging deeply into the red. But we continued to try these kinds of shows that first year, until we realized that they were always going to be a big bust.

During that year, each weekday, while anxiously anticipating and preparing more inventory for the next show, Judy and I discussed whether our craft was marketable and what it was that we were doing wrong. We reviewed and relived everything we were doing and agonized over whether our craft was good enough and whether there was a better way.

What we finally came to understand, after about fifteen of these kinds of shows, was that taking the advice of all those nice people who we had never met before and knew nothing about, was the only thing we were doing wrong. They

were so helpful and sincere that we couldn't resist following their recommendations, particularly when we had no idea where else to go.

Fact! We were doing everything right, *except* applying to the right shows.
The shows we were entering had cheap entry fees and no jury process involved,
so we thought we were saving money. We weren't taking into account the financial realities of the real-life crafts business world.

Harriet sold ticky-tacky, knickknack items. Her highest-priced item was
$10. She was applying to shows in a depressed economic area and that price
range was right in the customers' ballpark. Harriet grossed $300 a show and,
for her, that was a "great show." All that Harriet really wanted was a nice, pleasant, social day out in the park, where she earned a few extra dollars.

Joe sold wooden toys for small children, all also in a low price range. In the
really small towns where we were trying to sell, we didn't realize that a craft
show was a big event. It was a family day out in the local park or community
center, where the show was traditionally staged. There would be a few hundred
children running around and through the booths most of the day, pestering their
parents (particularly Daddy, as Daddys give in more easily) to buy them a toy
wooden gun or train or truck or whatever. Eventually Daddy would succumb to
the kid's pressure. At the end of two days, Joe maybe grossed $500 and, given
his cost of production and expenses, Joe has also had a "great show."

Edna sold junk jewelry, basically in the same price range, and she did fine.
We came to the show with our baskets ranging from $15 to $45. Kids weren't
screaming for Mommy to buy them a basket. Mommy could only afford to treat
herself to a cheap bracelet. So we grossed $350 and went home with long faces.
Oh, everyone loved our stuff and "wished" that they could buy it, but they simply could not afford it, and we simply shouldn't have been doing a show in that
town—or any town like it.

Our tip from this scenario is to remember to investigate the general economic conditions of the area in which you intend to do a show. Keep in mind that
the bigger your business becomes, the higher your expenses—and your expectations. If you persist long enough in doing shows of the kind I have described,
very soon you won't have any business at all—unless you are Edna or Joe or
Harriet and that is all you desire financially. Sometimes the problem is really
embarrassing. We did a show in Palm Springs, while visiting Judy's parents. We
expected a good show to be a bonus. We set up with our line of baskets and
found ourselves in a fine arts show, surrounded by $5,000 original paintings and
$10,000 statuary. Palm Springs is hardly the place to bring wooden baskets, no
matter how beautiful. We didn't belong in Palm Springs and we should not have
been accepted into the show.

Unfortunately, you'll have to live with the fact that there are a few
unscrupulous promoters who will accept anybody, if it enables them to fill

another space in their show and collect another booth fee. This fact is becoming a real threat to the craft industry. This kind of promoter was rare when we started in the business, but three veteran promoters told me that monetary greed on the part of new promoters is a serious concern. If you are accepted to a show on the basis of your application alone, it usually means that the promoter is accepting you sight unseen, and generally it is not a show worth doing. But more about that in a later chapter.

Judy and I did learn something important, however, from this early experience—besides what shows to avoid. We used the opportunity to discuss our craft with the customers who walked in and out of our booth. Their positive reactions to and comments about our product convinced us that we had a product that would sell, and that helped us maintain our confidence level. We learned that we just had to do a better job of selecting the shows we chose to attend.

A Great Show Is a Relative Matter

Perhaps, before I take you any further into this subject, we need to examine that phrase I keep using: "It's a great show." Remember Harriet and Edna and Joe? Well, they weren't lying to us when they said, "It's a great show." They were absolutely serious. The fact that we did not realize, or take into consideration, was that what may be a poor, good, or great show is purely subjective. Please remember that, and only under special circumstances put much stock in a strange vendor's advice. One person's "great show" is another person's "flop."

It is vitally important that you keep in mind that you know nothing about another craftsperson's operating expenses, much less his lifestyle, living expenses, or general expectations and philosophy concerning the crafts business. You will see many, many craftspeople who travel from show to show the entire crafts season, working in and living out of the small van in which they travel. Some began back in the sixties and have an entirely different philosophy of life than you may have. Many are quite content to make just enough money to pay their expenses week to week. They live hand-to-mouth. If that is all that you desire, you probably don't need to read the rest of this book.

The largest majority of craftspeople depend on the crafts business as their only source of income. Some are single and have only themselves to support. Others support large families; in fact, their business is a huge, family enterprise, involving brothers and sisters and cousins. Every relative works in the business. At shows like Country Folk Art, which is a nationwide organization based in Michigan, or Harvest Festival, a huge, top-of-the-line enterprise based in Petaluma, California, you will see craftspeople who roll up in fancy motor homes followed by two or three eighteen-wheelers. They travel with a staff who will actually put their wares together and keep their booth filled as their merchandise sells. A $25,000 gross for three days, may be a "poor" weekend for them and you'll hear them griping.

Still other craftspeople don't even travel with their booth or merchandise. When they are booked for the entire season with the Harvest Festival, for example—which primarily sponsors shows in the Midwest and the western United States—their booth display and merchandise is loaded on trucks by the show's staff and shipped on to the next show site. These crafts professionals either return home between shows to manufacture more merchandise or, more likely, have a staff at home manufacturing the product and shipping it to wherever the next show is scheduled. Most of these people started out small, just as some of you are doing, then expanded under circumstances that will be discussed in a later chapter.

Obviously, for crafts businesses that operate on this large a scale, the perception of a "great show" is going to be vastly different from yours. I don't want to make a cynic of you, because most people in the business are sincere in the advice they are trying to give you. You just have to keep in mind that their recommendations simply may not apply to you.

Then There Is the Liar

As in any other part of life and in every business, there are a few less-than-ethical types who have an axe to grind and will give out misleading and erroneous advice. Such a craftsperson regards every dollar spent in your booth as a dollar less spent in his. In economics, this philosophy is referred to as the *zero sum* concept, the idea that there is a finite amount of money to be divided up among everybody. Some people in the business view all competition from that standpoint and so will steer you away from any good show, particularly if you have a product in the same category as theirs. You will be told that a show is rotten, simply to reduce the competition. So be wary. Get more than one opinion.

As you do in every area of your life, learn to evaluate whom you can trust and whom you can't. When the person touting a show is someone you respect and who himself produces a fine product, then the recommendation is usually worth taking. A good craftsman wants good competition, because such competition makes for a higher-quality show. This, in turn, draws greater attendance and a more discriminating customer; plus, it stimulates spending.

If you produce a good product, you needn't be afraid of good competition. Good competition brings in more customers to the show. That is why a promotion like Harvest Festival or Country Folk Art, or similar top promotions in your part of the country, encourage and represent a level of craftsmanship and competition that you should strive to attain—even if you don't choose to apply to these particular shows. You may not wish to, and you don't necessarily need to, sell at the larger shows to make a good living. Many, many successful craftspeople never do shows at that level. However, those kinds of shows still represent the theoretical top, the ideal. Their criteria for who they will accept into their shows is quite strict, but if you make it, you know you're among the best in the business.

We cite the taking-recommendations-from-just-about-everybody method outlined above to demonstrate that this approach is, arguably the worst way to decide where to sell your merchandise. Listening to everyone and anyone—just because they make a craft and set up a booth—will get you someplace and no place at the same time. Word of mouth is a hit-or-miss proposition. It is highly unreliable financially, and it gives you no ability to assess a projected income upon which you can depend and continue to invest in your business. If you proceed only on the basis of a craftsperson's recommendations, we can predict with assurance that you will just eke out a living, making very little profit and will most likely become discouraged and quit. You cannot plan a show schedule a year in advance by acting on recommendations.

More Conventional Means of Selecting Your Shows

Another means of learning about which shows are being presented is one to which all craftspeople are subjected. It is the direct invitation that you will receive in the mail and, like every other option in this aspect of the crafts business, it has its advantages and disadvantages. Two such typical, unsolicited invitations can be found on the following pages. Particularly note that while there are numerous rules and regulations by which you must abide, the promoter is not even asking to see your product. To get into the show, you just have to fill out the application and send in your money.

These mailed invitations promoting a show will usually start arriving after you have been in the business a short while and out there displaying your product at some shows. Either some promoter has walked the show and has seen your work, or he has purchased a mailing list containing your name from one of your suppliers. These mailed invitations must be considered very carefully and, once you are established for a few years, most often rejected for reasons to be explained subsequently.

Another very frequent occurrence that presents you with an opportunity to select a few new shows is the promoter who walks into your booth with an application in his hand. This is the personal approach. At many of the bigger shows, you rarely see and may never meet the promoter, much less receive a direct, personal invitation. In this case, the promoter is virtually guaranteeing you a place in his show. Most often, you will and should forget about doing this show, for reasons also to be explained.

Negatives about the Unsolicited or Personal Invitation

You can bet on this: When some promoter either mails you an invitation to take part in his craft show or he personally walks into your booth and places an

General Information
Rules and Regulations

Send all applications to:

5th Annual Car Show/Craft Faire
People's Christian Fellowship

1. Make checks payable to P C F.

2. You may request 2 booths if necessary. Please indicate on applications.

3. You may request either indoor or outdoor booths, however you must indicate which you prefer. Indoor booth space is limited and will be on a first come, first serve basis.

4. You may reserve 1 or 2 chairs. If needed please indicate on application.

5. You may reserve a table at an additional charge. Please indicate on application and include the $5.00 fee in your check.

6. Each booth/car registration will receive a total of 2 free lunch passes redeemable at our food center.

7. 2 name tags will be provided for each booth registered.

8. Each registered booth will receive 1 free ticket for the drawings.

9. We cannot permit live animals either for sale or as part of the display.

10. Only vendor names which appear on the application will be permitted to display / sell items from each booth.

11. There is NO overnight parking.

12.   We will NOT permit: Any sexual connotations on items.
                                           Any obscene language on any item.
                                           Any occult symbols, i.e., trolls fairies, wizards,
                                           devils, new age items, crystals or any items deemed to be
                                           "like" the aforementioned items, or any other inappropriate
                                           materials for a church.

13.   There will also be: No smoking inside the church
                                           No alcoholic beverages
                                           No drugs
                                           No pets except for seeing eye dogs

14. Set up time will be from 7:00 AM to 9 AM.

15. P C F and the Car Show Vendor Committee reserves the right to refuse to rent to any vendor deemed necessary for a successful car show.

All Booth Applications must be received by May 15th.
If you have any further questions please call the church office.

invitation in your hands, he is probably a brand-new promoter just finding his way into the business.

When you are new yourself, hunting around for shows, rejected by others to whom you have applied, and you're becoming anxious because your future income is becoming very problematical, or you have a free weekend, or last week's show was a loser, it is very tempting to accept these kinds of invitations. Under these conditions, almost every craftsperson is susceptible to the flattery that this invitation represents.

The in-the-mail invitation you receive is tempting because you don't have to do any work finding this show. Flashing before your eyes is all that profit you are going to make and it is sitting in your mailbox, just waiting for you. All you have to do is fill out the application, mail it in with your fee (usually less that the big shows), show up, and sell your product. You know nothing about the area in which you are going to sell or the kind of people to whom you are going to sell. You especially don't know anything about the promoter, his or her motivations, ability, or the show's reputation. But you go because the whole process is so easy. We know, because we succumbed to this temptation—and got financially stung almost every time we did so.

The promoter who walks into your booth and presents an offer can make himself even more attractive. This promoter, in presenting you with his application, always makes it sound as if he has eyeballed every booth in the show and has selected just a chosen few of quality to invite to his show. How nice that he has appreciated your work and chosen you.

The actual fact is that this promoter has approached everyone, in every booth in the show, or, if the proprietor wasn't there, left his application on the counter. This promoter had to approach you this way because he is definitely aware that most experienced artisans have already scheduled their shows for the entire year.

If this individual's show had any previous reputation, it would be in some craft show guide or on some craft show schedule published in your part of the country. The promoter wouldn't have to be out soliciting your attendance. You would be sending for his application. So, this promoter's real appeal has to be to newcomers who are just learning about the crafts business, as is he. In this scenario, you will find that the show date is coming up soon and the spaces aren't filled. This alone is a bad sign. It suggests that many veteran craftspeople are either not anxious to do this show or don't even know about it. Therefore, never make an immediate commitment. You should just politely take the application, explaining that you have to review your show schedule. Then ask around about the promoter. If veteran craftspeople haven't heard of him, then the person is not a promoter of any note. Very frequently, you will find that the application presented to you at a show will be for a show scheduled in the very near future or even the following weekend. Again, the reason the promoter is soliciting you is that he hasn't filled all the booth spaces in his show. For any number of practical reasons, if you sign up for the show, you'll waste a weekend doing it, conclude it was a flop, and drive home disgusted.

In the process of going through this, you'll learn that the promoter was on a small budget, hadn't advertised well, was running the show in some godforsaken spot that was all he could rent, and the show had no history behind it to attract repeat customers. If you hadn't applied to it, you probably wouldn't have missed a thing. In fact, your time would have been better spent staying home and producing more inventory.

After you have been in business for a few years and you have established your reputation with recognized promoters, you will be on their mailing list every year and you will receive an application and schedule of every show they are promoting the coming year. You will receive the schedules well in advance of the approaching craft season and have plenty of time to make your decisions and apply for the shows. In this case, the promoter has in the past already seen your work and, to some extent, knows you and wants what your craft represents in his show. Two examples of these applications that we still receive are found on the following pages. Many craftspeople base their entire season on selecting all the shows done by just one or two major promoters. They are also usually rewarded for this by being given better booth locations at that promoter's shows.

Some craftspeople are even willing to do some promoters' poorer shows (that is, those in a poorer location) just to ensure that they are accepted into the good ones. Some in the crafts business might even recommend this approach, but we wouldn't. There are too many good shows around to waste time at any poor ones.

The Exception to the Rule

Here is the other side of the coin with regard to those unsolicited show invitations. The new promoter may be good at what she does, but has no track record as yet, and is advertising a "first annual." The "first annual" can present you with a very troubling dilemma.

As happened to us, the "first annual" that we chose not to attend turned out to be a huge success. All the craftspeople who took the risk not only made money but also virtually guaranteed themselves a spot in the next year's show because the promoter repaid them for taking the gamble. Having ignored the invitation, our chances of getting into next year's show were seriously reduced.

I hate to think of the money that some of our mistakes cost us. Judy and I turned down the First Annual Asparagus Festival in Stockton, California, years ago. I stupidly talked my wife out of doing it because I didn't think the people of

The Lake Tahoe Charities
PO BOX 158
KINGS BEACH, CA 96143

Truckee Regional Park
Arts and Crafts Fair
August 28 & 29

JURYING DEADLINE
Must be received
by April 1, 1999

BOOTH SIZES & FEES

10'x10' (10ft frontage)	$160.00
15'x10' (15ft frontage)	$225.00
20'x10' (20ft frontage)	$290.00

NAME: _____

BUSINESS NAME: _____

ADDRESS: _____CITY: _____

STATE: _____ZIP: _____PHONE #: _____Email #: _____

CA RESALE #_____CAR LICENSE, MAKE, STATE _____

I WILL BE SELLING:_____

_____

_____

SPACE SIZE_____

IF APPLICATION IS INCOMPLETE, IT WILL BE NOT BE JURIED

Enclosed is my NON-REFUNDABLE and NON-TRANSFERABLE, upon acceptance, entry fee, 5 PHOTOS OF MY CURRENT WORK AND 1 OF MY DISPLAY, A BUSINESS SIZE SELF ADDRESSED ENVELOPES with at least .55 postage. Please make your check payable to the Lake Tahoe Charities. There will be a $20 charge on all returned checks.

I agree to hold the Lake Tahoe Charities, the Truckee Donner Public Utility District, and Beth Weber, harmless for any and all liability of injury and damage to life and property. By signing this application, you are agreeing that you have read and will abide by all of the rules.

SIGNATURE_____DATE:_____

1999 HARVEST FESTIVAL
APPLICATION/CONTRACT
Please print with ballpoint pen

Harvest Festival/Southex
601 N. McDowell Blvd.
Petaluma, CA 94954-2312
(707)778-6300 or outside CA (800)321-1213
Fax (707)763-5346

❑ Previously Juried Exhibitor ID# _____

❑ First Time Applicant-Never Juried

Last Name _____ First Name _____

Firm Name _____

Directory *Name* Listing _____

Address _____

City _____ State _____ Zip _____

Phone (___)_____ Fax (___)_____

E-mail address _____

Seller Permit Numbers		
State/City	Number	
1. **California:**	_____	
2. **Arizona:**	_____	

Partner _____

Phone (___) _____ Fax (___) _____

Craft (*if different*):_____

CRAFT INFORMATION: Use the Jury Criteria form for craft process description. **Please list the items you will have for sale:**

_____
_____
_____

One word that best identifies your craft category: Jewelry, Country, Furniture, etc.:

Average retail price range for products: From $ _____ to $ _____

Shows Requested: Please fill in booth type and location using the information on the opposite page

Date	City	Type	Location
Aug. 27-29	Las Vegas		
Sept. 4-6	Long Beach		
Sept. 10-12	Phoenix		
Sept. 17-19	Del Mar		
Sept.24-26	Pleasanton		
Oct. 1-3	Ventura		
Oct. 1-3	Sacramento		
Oct. 15-17	San Diego		
Oct. 22-24	Anaheim		
Nov 5-7	Tucson		
Nov.12-14 & 19-21	San Francisco		
Nov. 26-28	San Jose		
Dec. 3-5	Pomona		

Include Full Deposit with Application

# of Shows _____ x $200 per standard booth,
_____ x $300 per 15' booth
_____ x $400 per 20' booth

= Deposit_____ ($400 per standard SF booth)

Method of Payment: Amount: $ _____
❑ Check ❑ Money Order
❑ Visa ❑ Mastercard
❑ Discover Card

Credit Card# _____
Exp. Date ___/___
(Contract signature verifies credit card)

Make checks payable to: **SOUTHEX EXHIBITIONS**
No postdated checks please
Monies will be deposited upon placement

I/We hereby apply for exhibit space in the 1999 Harvest Festival. I/We hereby agree to abide by the show terms, conditions, and regulations printed on the reverse side of this form. I/We agree to allow Harvest Festival to use my photo/video in all advertising campaigns. **Please make a copy of this contract for your records.**

Your Signature _____ Date _____

Conditions of Application/Contract

1. EXHIBITOR COVENANTS

a) The exhibitor agrees to abide by all rules and regulations adopted by Southex Exhibitions Inc. (a dmg Exhibition Group company) and sponsors and agrees that Southex Exhibitions Inc. shall have the final decision in adopting any rule or regulation deemed necessary prior to, during and after the show.

b) The exhibitor agrees to observe all union contracts and labor relations agreements in force, agreements between Southex Exhibitions Inc. and the official contractors serving the show facility and companies operating in the building in which the show is taking place and to observe the labor laws of the jurisdiction in which the building is located. The exhibitor will not do anything directly or indirectly connected with their display which might be a violation of any laws, bylaws, ordinances or regulations of any government or regulatory body.

c) The exhibitor agrees to obtain, at its own expense, any licenses or permits which are required, including without limitation, from government bodies, trade or industry associations, and any other third parties, for the operation of its trade or business during the show and to pay all taxes that may be levied against it as a result of the operation of its trade or business in their space allocated.

d) The exhibitor agrees not to conduct or be associated with a promotional contest in connection with the show, where a prize or prizes having a value in excess of $50 are offered, unless the exhibitor (i) satisfies Southex Exhibitions Inc. that the contest is being operated in accordance with law and (ii) provides a letter of credit or other security satisfactory to Southex Exhibitions Inc. covering the value of the prize(s).

e) The exhibitor agrees to obey any non-smoking regulations in effect at the facility and agrees to ensure that its officers, agents, employees, and those for whom in law they are responsible for, obey any such regulations.

f) It is the sole obligation of the Producer to furnish above exhibit space plus general lighting, cleaning of common area, heating and guard service. All other services of any nature shall be ordered in advance by the Exhibitor on forms provided.

2. DISPLAY

a) The exhibitor agrees to occupy the contracted exhibit space during the full term of the show and to exhibit only the products described in this contract.

b) Southex Exhibitions Inc. reserves the right, in its sole and unfettered discretion to: (i) determine the eligibility of exhibitors and exhibits for the show, (ii) reject or prohibit exhibits or exhibitors which Southex Exhibitions Inc. considers objectionable, and (iii) relocate exhibitors or exhibits when in Southex Exhibitions Inc.'s opinion such moves are necessary to maintain the character and/or good order of the show.

c) Exhibitor agrees that, if accepted, Producer is under no obligation to rent space to Exhibitor in future years. Booth locations will be rented and assigned in accordance with the best interest of the exposition, which Producer in its sole discretion shall have the right to decide. Southex will not give any exhibitor exclusivity on a product.

d) **Absolutely NO IMPORTED ITEMS. Franchise organization or products bought and resold will NOT be allowed.** Any exhibitor found displaying or selling such items in their booth may be asked to vacate immediately from said booth with no refund of booth fees. All work submitted must be handmade by the applicant in North America.

3. ASSIGNMENT AND SUBLETTING

The exhibitor shall not assign any rights under this agreement or sublet the space without the prior written permission of Southex Exhibitions Inc. which permission may be arbitrarily withheld.

4. INSURANCE

The exhibitor shall obtain and maintain at its own expense during the period commencing on the first move-in date and terminating on the last move-out date, a policy of insurance acceptable to Southex Exhibitions Inc.. The policy of insurance shall name Southex Exhibitions Inc. as loss-insured and insure the exhibitor against all claims of any kind arising from or in any way connected with the exhibitor's presence or operations at the show. Policy shall provide coverage of at least $1,000,000 for each separate occurrence. At the request of Southex Exhibitions Inc., the exhibitor shall provide Southex Exhibitions Inc. with a copy of such policy.

5. INDEMNITY

a) The exhibitor accepts all risks associated with the use of the exhibit space and environs. The exhibitor shall not make any claim or demand or take any legal action, whatsoever, against Southex Exhibitions Inc., the show sponsors or the facility in which the show is held, for any loss, damage or injury howsoever caused, to the exhibitor, its officers, employees, agents or their property.

b) The exhibitor agrees to indemnify and hold harmless Southex Exhibitions Inc., show sponsors and the facility, their respective officers, agents and employees, against all claims, costs and charges of every kind resulting from their occupancy of the exhibit space or its environs, for personal injuries, death, property damages or any other damage sustained by the exhibitor or its officers, agents, employees or those for whom in law they are responsible, or Southex Exhibitions Inc. or a visitor to the show.

6. EXHIBITOR'S PROPERTY

All of the exhibitor's property at the show shall be at the sole risk of the exhibitor and Southex Exhibitions Inc. assumes no responsibility for loss or damage thereto.

7. BUILDING

The exhibitor is liable for any damage they cause to the facility or to any property of Southex Exhibitions Inc., its agents or any other exhibitor. The exhibitor may not apply paint, lacquer, adhesive or other coatings to the facility or to the property of Southex Exhibitions Inc., its agents or any other exhibitor.

8. PAYMENT TERMS, CANCELLATION, AND TERMINATION

a) A deposit of $200 per standard booth is required for each show requested with the application; $400 for San Francisco. The balance is due and payable in full on or before July 30, 1999. No booth assignments will be given unless deposits or full booth payments are received with the completed application. Any booths not paid in full by July 30 are subject to cancellation without a refund. Past due balances, on approved credit, greater than 30 days, beginning 7/30/99 are charged 1.5% per month service charge until the balance is paid in full. After 7/30/99, 100% of the booth fee is due with applications, any additional shows or booth increases.

b) Prior to 7/30 no fee if cancellation is made **within 10 days of 1st statement.** After the 10 day grace period, a cancellation fee equal to your deposit will be charged if the cancellation is before 7/30/99. The 10 day grace period does not apply after July 30. **Cancellation after 7/30/99 will result in 100% of the booth fee being forfeited.**

c) In the event the exhibitor fails to make payment as aforesaid or fails to comply in any respect with the terms of this contract, Southex reserves the right to cancel this contract without notice and all rights of the exhibitor hereunder shall cease and terminate. Any payment made by the exhibitor on account hereof will be retained by show management as liquidated damages for breach of his contract and show management may thereupon Rent said space. Failure to appear at the event does not release exhibitor from responsibility for payment of the full cost of the space rented.

9. REMOVAL OF EXHIBITS

The exhibitor agrees no display will be dismantled or goods removed during the entire run of the show, but will remain intact until the end of the final closing hour of the last show day. The exhibitor also agrees to remove its display and equipment from the show site by the final move-out time limit, or in the event of failure to do so, the exhibitor agrees to pay for such additional cost as may be incurred.

10. CANCELLATION OR CURTAILMENT OF SHOW

In the event that the facility in which the show is to be held or is held is destroyed or becomes unavailable for occupancy, for reasons beyond the control of Southex Exhibitions Inc. and sponsors, or if for any reason Southex Exhibitions Inc. is unable to permit the exhibitor to occupy the facility or the space, or if the show is canceled or curtailed, Southex Exhibitions Inc. and sponsors will not be responsible for any loss of business, loss of profits, damage or expense of whatever nature that the exhibitor may suffer. The reasons listed include, but are not limited to, such reasons as: casualty, explosion, fire, lightning, flood, weather, epidemic, earthquake or other Acts of God, acts of public enemies, riots or civil disturbances, strike, lockout or boycott.

11. NSF CHECKS

In the event that the exhibitor's check is returned by a bank due to insufficient funds, **a $25 administration fee will be charged to the exhibitor.**

Stockton would turn out. I missed the fact that the promoter was an experienced veteran, not a newcomer to the business. The show drew 100,000 people the first year and thousands more than that as the show grew in popularity and became a local, established tradition. Thereafter, craftspeople from all over the state of California and beyond were applying. Everyone wants to be part of a big success. That mistake on my part resulted in our never being accepted into the show after that first year, and after a number of years, we finally stopped applying. I never heard the end of it.

There is no right or absolute answer to how to make some of these decisions. It depends on how many shows you are doing, how many more you want to do, your financial status, the amount of inventory you have in stock, how much more you can manufacture, and how hard you want to and are physically capable of working. Then you just have to weigh the odds, make your decision, and live with it.

In fact, you may decide to participate in a "first annual" being put on by a new, inexperienced promoter, and it may turn out to be a great show. Every show is always a gamble to some extent. That is just the nature of the business. We can only give you lessons from our experience, and remind you to try to keep the odds in your favor—and hope.

The Best Method of Selecting Your Shows

If you're a novice or a veteran to this business, far and away the best method of selecting the shows you will try to do is by subscribing to whatever crafting guide exists in your locale, state, or area of the country. Every craftsperson I have ever met subscribes to at least one, even when they have a long, established schedule that they do every year and are on the regular mailing list of dozens of promoters. People who sell their crafts at shows are always looking for new shows, always seeking to test new territory. These guides give you a better measure of the shows to which you want to apply than the gambling methods noted above, and they provide you the means by which you can plan your schedule much further in advance than the above examples.

There are good, practical reasons to always be on the lookout for new shows: First and foremost, no matter how good your product, you can saturate a given area by appearing there too often. Suburban areas extending outside the big cities, sometimes called the "suburban sprawl," are good examples.

Most of suburbia is a series of once–small towns that, years ago, were miles apart, but with continuing expansion in every direction, now run into each other. The result is that, except for the population sign entering each township or minicity, you can't tell one from the other. And yet, each area or town has a name and a history and each develops its own traditions.

One of those traditions is becoming the yearly craft show. It is often sponsored by the local Chamber of Commerce, and every community organization,
such as the Rotary, the Lions Club, the Elks, the Masons, and the Knights of
Columbus—all supporting charitable causes—dedicate their time and effort to
staging a successful show. It is a community enterprise and, in recent years,
these annual craft shows have developed into friendly, intercommunity compe-
titions, very often in support of some community project for which the town is
attempting to raise funds. Communities coordinate their efforts, so they usually do not hold their craft fair on the same weekend as a neighboring community, but there are just so many good weekends, so occasionally they will overlap.

In California, with so much of the state dedicated to agriculture, the last
fifteen years have seen the development of every conceivable fair and festival
celebrating some fruit or vegetable or nut. There's the Pear Fair, the Artichoke
Festival, Cherry Blossom Time, the Apple Hill Fair, the Asparagus Festival, the
Garlic Festival, the Walnut Festival, and on and on. Offhand, I can think of only
a few major fruits or vegetables or "nuts" that California *doesn't* raise—coconuts
and pineapples. You fill in the fruit or vegetable or nut and we have a show in its
honor. Amazingly, and thankfully, we don't yet have a Marijuana Festival! Every
one of these festivals includes a craft show. The problem with all these shows is
that while they give you a multiplicity of potential shows from which to select,
because they are so close together in time and geographical location, many of the
same potential customers show up at every one. People who love craft shows are
like people who stop at every garage sale. They provide a crowd and can be counted on to patronize every food and beverage booth, but they only have so much
money to spend on crafts. Whether you're in a highly paid yuppie community or
out in the farm belt with hundreds of migrant workers, craft show patrons still
operate on a budget. They can't afford to buy from you every week. The customers
stop by to say hello because they come to recognize you, and you them. It's all very
social, but it may not make you a lot of money.

Another reason to be looking for new shows is that you will inevitably experience the poor or losing show on which you gambled and lost. There are the
rained-out shows, the occasional cancelled show, due to some regional catastrophe
in the area like a fire or flood, or such devastating heat that nobody comes out to
the show. These occurrences reduce your potential gross income for the year, unless
you can find a good substitute for them on a open weekend. This is when you
become susceptible to signing up for those dicey shows that we discussed above.

Another problem you'll face is the potentially good show that the promoter just didn't advertise sufficiently. You, of course, have no control over this. You
can complain to the promoter when you find out about it, but that won't help you
that weekend. Next year, don't sign up for that promoter's shows. You will have
to learn from experience which promoters fudge on their budget in this way and

which do not. Other promoters do eventually draw only the most desperate craftspeople to their shows, and you want to avoid that scenario.

Yet, it is a scenario that may become too common. Beth Weber of North Tahoe Fine Arts Association, one of the most concerned and experienced promoters we know, told me, "The reality is that fewer promoters are coming into the business and the veterans are becoming more complacent and less discriminating." Hopefully, while that may be happening in California, it is not necessarily the case everywhere.

The Guide Book

Whatever the scenario that sends you searching for shows, either at the beginning of the year or throughout the year for the various and sundry reasons mentioned above, a craft guide is still the best way to find the shows at which you will have a better than average chance of making a profit. If you are wondering where you find these guides, ask your neighbors, at any show, and they will tell you what magazine they use and how to subscribe. Usually, they'll have a copy with them. Since we cannot speak to whether or not a guide can be found in every area of the country, you will have to research your own locale.

Certainly, you can find out what shows are taking place in your area from your local newspaper, local events calendars, and Sunday supplements. Magazines, like the one published by the California Automobile Association, or the many travel and camper magazines, also list events for the year throughout all parts of the country. However, these are not guides and will not give you all the information you need other than the date, time, and place of the shows. Like every other aspect of this business, however, even the best guide has its assets and its liabilities, and you have to learn how to use it properly. Here are a few tips and guidelines.

On the following pages you will find samples of a show guide that we used. It is called the *Crafts Fair Guide* and is published by Lee and Dianne Spiegle of Corte Madera, California. The first shows an application to subscribe to the *Guide*. The second explains how to use the *Guide*. At the time we were in business, it was arguably the most-used guide in California, Nevada, Oregon, and Arizona, and we believe it still is. Lee himself was a vendor, and his story is fascinating. It symbolizes and reflects the spirit of the craft world.

Twenty-five years ago, Lee was selling balloons at craft shows. The craft show industry was in its infancy then and craft shows were of very poor quality. Nobody really made any serious money and craftspeople were always complaining about promoters who lured them to shows that were often dismal financial failures. The next year those promoters would find new suckers to fill their spaces. Attendance was usually poor, and the quality of crafts questionable. There was no type of periodical or magazine that even listed potential

Looking for GREAT Shows?

Get the most powerful tool for choosing *successful* fairs...

THE CRAFTS FAIR GUIDE

WHAT IS IT?

THE CRAFTS FAIR GUIDE reviews approximately 1,000 fairs occurring throughout the West. Several thousand reviewers -- craftspeople like yourself -- send us a total of over 10,000 individual evaluations each year. THE CRAFTS FAIR GUIDE compiles those evaluations into a format that gives you the information you need to make the right choices about which fairs to select. *And* which to avoid.

That's important. Because if you pick enough bad fairs, you'll be out of business before you know it. And if you choose enough good ones, you and your business will thrive.
We're here for *YOU.*
Subscribing to THE CRAFTS FAIR GUIDE could make the difference between just getting by...and getting ahead. That's not a tough choice.

HOW DOES IT WORK?

Exhibitors review each fair, giving information on the date and location, the entry fee, site conditions, parking, the promoter's name and address, and *--most important--* rating sales on a scale of 0 to 10.

WHAT DOES IT COST?

THE CRAFTS FAIR GUIDE costs just $45 for a full year's subscription -- four large quarterly issues -- much less than the cost of doing just ONE bad show.

WHAT DO PEOPLE SAY ABOUT THE SHOWS?

Turn this page to see SAMPLE REVIEWS!

OUR GUARANTEE

The CRAFTS FAIR GUIDE is *unconditionally guaranteed* for the life of your subscription.

If, at any time, you don't feel that the Crafts Fair Guide is worth much more than you paid for it, just return your copies and we will *promptly* refund your $45.
No questions asked.
No hard feelings.

Lee

LEE SPIEGEL, *Editor & Publisher*
The Crafts Fair Guide
P.O. Box 688
Corte Madera, CA 94976

Okay, Lee ... Sign Me Up!   ☐ New Subscription   ☐ Subscription Renewal

I want to subscribe to THE CRAFTS FAIR GUIDE. Here is my $45.   Subscription No. _____

If I decide THE CRAFTS FAIR GUIDE is not for me, you'll promptly refund my money.

NAME _____
ADDRESS _____
CITY, STATE, ZIP _____ PHONE (____) _____
MC/VISA:* _____ EXP.: _____ SIG.: _____

SEND TO: THE CRAFTS FAIR GUIDE • P.O. BOX 688 • CORTE MADERA • CA 94976
*MasterCard & VISA accepted by phone/FAX : 415- 924-3259 • 800-871-2341

HOW TO USE
THE CRAFTS FAIR GUIDE

GENERAL INFORMATION

THE CRAFTS FAIR GUIDE is published quarterly, evaluating last year's fairs so you'll have a basis for choosing this year's. Each fair has been rated by one or more exhibitors, using the CFG Evaluation Form.

You'll find an overall description of each fair: the name, location, weather, and date; a description of the site; estimate of attendance; an average rating for the fair based on Sales and Enjoyability (S/E); and comments by the participants about the fair and the promoter.

When you decide which shows look good, look them up in the UPCOMING INFORMATION section for this year's information.

THE SALES GRAPH shows how many people rated the fair, their crafts, and their ratings on a scale of 0 (bad) to 10 (great).

EXAMPLE

```
0  1  2  3  4  5  6  7  8  9  10
                        P     P
                        J
```

INTERPRETATION:
One potter rated it a 10 (great). And a jeweler agreed. A second potter gave it a 9. This was a very good show for these three reviewers. The sales graph reflects only sales, not enjoyability.

THE CRAFTS CODES: It's not possible to assign a letter for every imaginable craft, so some categories are broader than others.

A – Paintings	M – Fiber Arts
a – Prints	N – Food
B – Batiks	O – Music
C – Country Crafts	P – Pottery
D – Florals and Plants	R – Xmas Crafts
E – Decorative/Tole	S – Soft Sculpture
F – Photography	T – Textile
G – Glass	t – Clothing
H – Sculpture	W– Woodwork
I – Ceramics	X – Mixed Media
J – Jewelry over $100	Y – No category/hard
j – Jewelry under $100	to define
K – Kidstuff	Z – Declined to state
L – Leather	

Following the Sales Graph will be craftspeoples' comments about the fair and promoter. The comments are in descending order and reflect the Sales Graph. The numbers in parentheses following each comment refer to the person's rating of the fair. If there are two numbers, they rate sales and enjoyability (5/8 means 5 for sales, 8 for enjoyment). With a three-number rating, the middle number indicates gross sales to the nearest $100 (5/6/8 would be the same rating, but would also tell you that this person had a $600 show).

DEADLINE AND SCHEDULE:
Send us reviews no later than two months after the fair has occurred, so that we can process them in a timely manner. Each issue is printed and in the mail several months before the shows occur.

ISSUE	MAILED
January-March	September 1
April-June	December 1
July-September	March 1
October-December	June 1

SOME HINTS

First, read this page. Front and back. It will give you a general picture of how the whole thing works. Then browse through THE GUIDE, looking at a variety of shows to get a feel for the kind of information THE GUIDE contains. Make a note of whatever seems unclear. And then, read this page again. Most of THE GUIDE is pretty easy to figure out, once you understand the basic system.

Notice how many people evaluated the fair you're investigating. The more, the better. If there are five or more reports, that's a pretty good sample. On the other hand, if there are just one or two reviews, the report could be unbalanced. The reviewer may have had an atypical experience with the fair or promoter.

The "Would You Return" question on the Evaluation Form is an important indicator of the quality of the show. If the majority of respondents said they'd do the show again, it's likely to be a good show for you, too. If the majority said they'd never go back, it might be a good idea to stay away.

Read the Sales Graph and Ratings. Look at the way the ratings are distributed. Are most of them on the high end? If so, then it was a good fair for most sellers. Just because a person in your craft gave the show a 10, while everyone else gave it a 2, don't assume that you'll have a 10 also. Most likely, you'll join the 2s. Of course, if all the potters gave ratings between 8 and 10, that's a good sign that this show is good for potters in general, even if jewelers died there.

Read the comments! There may be facts that aren't expressed in the graph, and there may be factors that give the ratings a different slant. The comments will also reveal that for one person a $200 show is fantastic, while for another anything less than $1000 is rotten.

Note the cost of the show. Compare this year to last year. Some shows may raise their fees considerably from one year to the next and, therefore, become less cost effective.

ABOUT THE COMMENTS:
The opinions in the reviews are not the opinions of the staff of The Guide. They are your opinions, and we want to accurately present your ideas and feelings in the reviews. We can't overemphasize the importance of your evaluations. Please try to send us an Evaluation Form for every show that you do as soon afterward as you can. We include Evaluation Forms with every issue. If you need more, let us know.
We usually print all comments about the fairs and the promoters. We feel that, out of the many different points of view, you get a better picture of what the show was like.
However, when there are many evaluations submitted for a show, we can suffer from too much of a good thing. Therefore, when we get more than 15 evaluation forms for the same show, we use all the ratings, but print just a representative sampling of the comments.
If a fair you're interested in doesn't appear, or if your review wasn't printed, there are three explanations:

1. We did not receive a review of that fair.
2. The information we received was insufficient or suspect.
3. The review(s) arrived after our deadline.

shows, much less any information about them—which to apply for and which to avoid. As Lee told me, "I saw a need and I filled it."

Lee started the *Crafts Fair Guide* to meet that need, and had only 300 subscribers the first year. While developing his new enterprise, Lee continued to sell balloons to cover the costs of the new business. Today, he still sells balloons from time to time to keep in touch with the customers, craftspeople, and the changing nature of the business. But today he also has 25,000 subscribers who pay $45 a year for his guide. That story represents the true entrepreneurial spirit of America—and, by the way, should give you some idea of the extent of the competition you face in the crafts business. Imagine how many craftspeople are setting up their booths every weekend, all over the country!

A good guide, like Lee's, will give you the location of shows and the weekend they were held *last* year. I have emphasized last year, because most established promotions book their shows for approximately the same weekend, year after year, just as each show also establishes its yearly tradition. However, dates can never be exactly the same year to year, so until you apply, you will only know the approximate weekend.

Lee's guide and most like it will specify the name of the promoter, the location and date of the show, and where to mail your application. You will not, however, be making your application choices just on that basis. The real bonus of Lee's guide is that you'll find evaluations of every show, by any craftsperson who cared to submit an evaluation, either by handing it in at the end of the show or by mailing the form to the publisher of the guide. That evaluation will be printed in next year's guide and you will receive the guide months prior to your having to apply to any show. Just flipping through the guide will be an eye-opener to you, when you realize just how many shows are going on every weekend. An example of the evaluation form submitted by craftspeople is also on the following pages.

Sometimes, perhaps only one artisan may have submitted an evaluation, but more often you will have the opportunity to read the comments of six or eight participants in the show; for the really big shows, as many as fifty people may submit their appraisal of last year's show. So most of the time you will get a pretty fair, objective, and quite varied opinion of the show on which to base your decision as to whether to apply or not.

The information contained in the evaluation form is very specific. Every type of craft is listed under a category designation such as wood, wood and fabric, ceramics, pottery, jewelry, and the like, and each is assigned a letter. When you have chosen your category and letter designation, you just refer to those evaluations that fall within your category.

These evaluations give you a rough idea of what you might expect if you sold at that show. Just remember, though; it is a *rough* idea. Maybe another per-

THE FAIR EVALUATION FORM

CITY _____ NAME OF FAIR/MALL _____

DATE(S)*** _____ DAY(S) M T W T F S S | ***Reviews must be received within 2 months of the show.

ENVIRONMENT: ❑ INSIDE ❑ OUTSIDE DESCRIBE: _____

_____

_____

DESCRIBE PUBLIC: (e.g. Browsers, Sophisticated, Families, etc.)_____

WEATHER: _____

COST: $ _____ &/OR _____ % IF PERCENTAGE, CENTRAL CASHIER? YES _____ NO _____ PUBLIC'S COST: _____

1. HOW DO YOU RATE THIS FAIR FOR SALES? (BAD) 0 1 2 3 4 5 6 7 8 9 10 (GREAT)

1a. (Optional) APPROXIMATE GROSS, TO THE CLOSEST $100: 0 1 2 3 4 5 6 7 8 9 10 11 12 13 14 15 16 17 18 19 20 21

22 23 24 25 26 27 28 29 30 31 32 33 34 35 36 37 38 39 40 41 42 43 44 45 46 47 48 49 50 52 54 56 58 60 _____

2. HOW DO YOU RATE THIS FAIR FOR ENJOYABILITY? 0 1 2 3 4 5 6 7 8 9 10

3. WOULD YOU RETURN? YES _____ NO _____ ? _____ 4. ATTENDANCE: LOW _____ MEDIUM _____ HIGH _____

5. COMMENTS ABOUT THE FAIR IN GENERAL: _____

_____

_____

6. PROMOTER: _____ PHONE: (_____) _____

PROMOTER'S ADDRESS: _____

7. COMMENTS ABOUT THE PROMOTER: _____

_____

_____

_____

8. WHAT IS YOUR CRAFT? _____ IF JEWELER, WHAT PRICE CATEGORY? UNDER $100 _____ OVER $100 _____
   (LETTER SYMBOL IF KNOWN)

Every 3 months a FAIR EVALUATION FORM is picked at random in a drawing for a FREE year's

subscription toTHE CRAFTS FAIR GUIDE. To be eligible, please fill in the form below.

NAME _____ PHONE: (_____) _____

ADDRESS: _____

CITY _____ STATE _____ ZIP _____

ABOUT THE CRAFTS FAIR GUIDE

The CRAFTS FAIR GUIDE reviews and evaluates over 1000 fairs throughout the West. We compile data from
over 10,000 Evaluation Forms like this one into concise, easy-to-use quarterly magazines that give you the
information you need to decide which fairs to do... and which ones to avoid.

REMEMBER: Doing good fairs while avoiding bad ones is the key to getting ahead in the crafts fair business.
A full year's subscription to The Crafts Fair Guide is just $45...far less than the cost of doing ONE bad fair.

OUR UNCONDITIONAL GUARANTEE: If, at any time, you are not entirely satisfied with your subscription, just
return your copies, and we'll promptly refund your money.

Thanks for your help.
Please send this form to:
THE CRAFTS FAIR GUIDE
P.O. BOX 688
CORTE MADERA, CA 94976
PHONE OR FAX: 415-924-3259 / 800-871-2341
To FAX: Press "Send" after first ring.
	I'm not a CFG subscriber _____.
	   Send me Subscription Information _____.
	I'm a CFG subscriber _____.
	   Send me _____ Evaluation Forms.
	   Send me _____ Subscription Forms to give to others.

Evalform

son's product isn't made as well as yours or maybe it's better. Perhaps their "wood" is furniture and yours is much less expensive rustic shelves that are in greater demand; or maybe one respondent's customer relations skills are not as polished as yours. A sample page of typical commentary by craftspeople who participated in a previous year's show is reprinted on the following page.

Be that as it may, according to their category of craft, the merchants who submit their evaluations will give an approximation of their gross income and an evaluation or description of the setup conditions (long haul, rough terrain, many stairways, no elevators, etc.), nature of the crowd, general weather conditions to be expected, opinion on the promoter, and whatever gripes they may have, real or imagined. They will comment about practically any phase of the show operation, including whether or not there were enough toilet facilities, whatever entertainment was provided, and the quality of the food. Some evaluations are so creative and humorous that we have sometimes wondered if they and we were at the same show. However, most evaluations are devastatingly honest, and only you are in a position to judge how all the information applies to you.

When you are a beginner and trying to use the various guides for the first time, you have very little experience on which to base a judgment. I know that the first year we used them, Judy and I tended to treat the guides as gospel truth. We learned better over the years, for reasons I'll later explain, but as a rough guide, they serve very well.

Particularly, note how much money that the craftspeople in your category *say* they earned. Then compare it with their evaluations. Note the category for *sales,* and determine if it squares with the crafters' stated price range and, therefore, whether the evaluators really could have earned what they said they earned. Pay particular attention to whether everyone's sales were generally what you would consider high, and what you are aiming to make, or whether only specific categories earned high ratings. That can tell you something about buyer taste in that area.

Most evaluators are scrupulously honest. But there are some, as in every walk of life, who for a variety of reasons, will misrepresent their earnings at a given show. They may have done poorly for any number of reasons that have nothing to do with the promotion itself. According to the promoters with whom I discussed this subject, if craftspeople do poorly at a show, the first person they will always blame is the promoter. It is just something that promoters learn to live with. In reality, a craftsperson's failure may have had nothing to do with the promoter.

Craftspeople who have spent years in the business may make comments based on prejudices, personal inadequacies, or hidden agendas. In some cases, they may just want to stifle the competition, so they write a poor evaluation of vendor's lunch orders. Nice." (6/10/6) ◆◆◆ "Did a good job, except that there were only 2 porta-potties and they were a mess. Some people told me they would like to see more artists in the show." (5/3/5) ◆◆◆ "She says she advertises, but putting a sign on the rear of your pickup isn't what we had in mind. She doesn't even accept personal checks." (1/1/3)

CA, SAN FRANCISCO: Sukkot – The Festival of the Booths
DATE(S): October 11, 1998
SETTING: On closed-off Arguello Street in front of Temple Emanu-El.
WEATHER: Sunny and mild.
COST: $125
ATTENDANCE: MEDIUM
WOULD YOU RETURN? Yes-6 No-2 ?-3

0	1	2	3	4	5	6	7	8	9	10	RATING:	6.1
	I	I	P	N			J	Y		J	S/E:	5.4/6.7
	J						i	Z				
								T				

COMMENTS ABOUT THE FAIR:
"Very small and charming. Crowd was very sophisticated and family-oriented. A few artists that I have never seen before. Excellent location and great crowd." (10/10) ◆◆◆ "All kinds in crowd. Very enjoyable. Great location." (8/5/10) ◆◆◆ "You name it, it was there. Expected the fair itself to be larger. I don't live in the area so I don't know what they did to promote it." (8/2) ◆◆◆ "Beautiful crafts; many high-ticket items did well. Had to haggle over price, but most were interested and bought. High ratio of buyers to lookers." (7/8/7) ◆◆◆ "Families. Nice. Some beautiful, high-quality merchandise and artists. Fun show. No pilferage. Nice folks. Need more food and drink. Only had Jewish food." (7/8/7) ◆◆◆ "Friendly, family crowd. Well organized. Great public." (7/7/7) ◆◆◆ "Well organized by promoter; however, not located in a high traffic area. One-day event for the Jewish holiday." (4/4/5) ◆◆◆ "Upper middle class crowd. About what we predicted. Not many sales, but okay for the amount of crowd. Artist behind me with Jewish products did well. Very hard parking definite drawback." (3/3/10) ◆◆◆ "More Jewish than I thought. Although it was a Sukkot fair, I thought the crowd would be more mixed. Most of the booths seemed to be Jewish." (2/2/6) ◆◆◆ "A lot of lookers; not many buyers." (2/3/3) ◆◆◆ "The fair had a reasonable number of educated, Jewish shoppers. This was handy since I sell Judaica." (1/1/7)
COMMENTS ABOUT THE PROMOTER:
(Terry Pimsleur & Co., See Promoters List): "Very nice and very available." (10/10) ◆◆◆ "Well organized." (8/5/10) ◆◆◆ "More attention to details needed. Great on the phone prior to the fair." (8/2) ◆◆◆ "Businesslike; checked out our artistic quality." (7/8/7) ◆◆◆ "Our first show with Pimsleur. We can't complain." (7/8/7) ◆◆◆ "Great." (7/7/7) ◆◆◆ "Well organized." (4/4/5) ◆◆◆ "Same as always." (3/3/10) ◆◆◆ "Okay; I didn't really deal with them." (2/2/6) ◆◆◆ "They did a good job as far as management is concerned." (2/3/3)

OR, EUGENE: ASUO Fall Street Fair
DATE(S): October 14-16, 1998
SETTING: Booths set up on both sides of 13th Street through U of O campus.
WEATHER: Rainy Wednesday and Thursday. Sunny and cool Friday.
COST: $90
ATTENDANCE: MEDIUM
WOULD YOU RETURN? Yes-5 No-3 ?-2

0	1	2	3	4	5	6	7	8	9	10	RATING:	4.6
t		G			Y	A	j				S/E:	3.6/5.5
		B			P							
		t				j						
		W										

COMMENTS ABOUT THE FAIR:
"Outside on busy walking thoroughfare on campus. Nice, casual atmosphere. Good mix of handcrafted and imported work. Super spot on campus, very central. Parking, however, was limited and difficult to find." (7/4/9) ◆◆◆ (6/4) ◆◆◆ "About two blocks long. Very casual, friendly vendors and open minded customers. Setting up was fairly easy." (5/4/10) ◆◆◆ "Student-priced work sells best. Some difficulty this year because of poor communication about fire regulations. Food is excellent. Traffic and location very good." (5/5/7) ◆◆◆ "This year we got hassled about tarps not being fire resistant. Weather was bad and students lacked funds. It's been better in the past." (5/8/5) ◆◆◆ "Good potential. Weather and time of year can be a problem." (2/3/10) ◆◆◆ "Fire marshal came around and harassed everyone." (2/4) ◆◆◆ (2/3) ◆◆◆ "Low-quality work for the most part. Street fair mentality." (2/5/2) ◆◆◆ "Customers mostly broke but friendly students. Had to accept post-dated checks to make sales. Loading and unloading great. Parking a nightmare. Fire marshal threatened to make me take down my umbrella tarp in the rain. Not juried. Many, many cheap imported clothing booths. $15 tie-dyed rayon dresses from Thailand in booth next to mine. Best food of any fair I've been to." (0/2/1)
COMMENTS ABOUT THE PROMOTER:
(Associated Students, Erb Memorial Union Suite 4, University of Oregon, Eugene, OR 97403): "Good communication, well organized. Few problems. Wish they had permanent base camp near to fair." (7/4/9) ◆◆◆ "Not very well organized. Should make sure fire regulation rules are clearly stipulated in vendor information. The harassment by fire officials was ridiculous." (6/4) ◆◆◆ "Because it's run by a student organization, management can vary from year to year. Also, student security volunteers are insufficiently strict with moving/removing guerilla vendors." (5/5/7) ◆◆◆ "Nice gal, but a bit overbearing about the tarps. Not her fault, and she tried hard not to make the ordeal too difficult for the vendors." (5/8/5) ◆◆◆ "Unyielding on some demands. Misinformation about booth setup. Bad parking." (2/3/10) ◆◆◆ "Best they can do with what they have to work with." (2/5/2) ◆◆◆ "Tiffany, the woman in charge, was pleasant but powerless against the fire marshal's bullying. Initially I was placed next to another tie-dyer. She moved me down a couple of booths. She was helpful and available most of the time. She returned phone calls. Did her best." (0/2/1)

the show. Or, perhaps they made more money than they reported to the promoter, if the show fee also included a percentage of their sales. Then, too, the craftsperson may just be hiding income from the IRS. So all you can do is find those evaluations by someone in the same product category as yours and then decide if what they say they earned is a figure that satisfies your needs. Of course, that still doesn't guarantee that you will make the same amount of money. Nothing and no one can guarantee that.

Many Factors Will Influence Your Show Selection

Ironically, with experience, you may also find yourself choosing not to do some shows that you know are excellent. Perhaps you decide against an outdoor show, where the weather is always poor, when you know of a show that's equally good but is held indoors and you don't have to deal with the weather factor. You also may decide that a show is just too far away, taking up too much travel time or costing too much in travel expenses. Sometimes, making less gross money is better than making more. Do your arithmetic.

Which shows you choose also depends on some simple, practical facts related to your particular life and lifestyle. Only you can determine this. Consider the following: how much cash reserve you have amassed from the preceding year, how hard you are willing to work, the amount of inventory you can afford to produce, and, finally, how far you are willing to travel.

When Judy and I began, we had a young son, Mark. We could take him anywhere. He thought the shows were a real treat, with playgrounds to romp in and new places to see. Missing a few days of school had no effect on his schoolwork, and we always had his teachers send us homework in advance.

As Mark grew older, however, just keeping him amused became a chore. I spent more time entertaining my son than I did selling in the booth. We would tour the show endlessly, go to a movie, do his homework, anything to keep him occupied. Eventually, of course, he could not miss school, and one of us had to stay home while the other did the shows alone—something that we swore we would never do. But now it was big business, and our viewpoint changed.

This put a totally different perspective on the shows. In our case, Judy was the logical choice to do the selling, as she is the better salesperson and could deal best with women—their decorating tastes, color schemes, and so on—and women constituted 98 percent of our customers. This was another forced choice. Furthermore, as our business became more and more successful, I had to stay home in order to produce enough inventory for the next show.

So much capital outlay was now involved that we could only afford to select the best shows where we, from experience, were relatively certain we would gross $3,000–$6,000 a show. The baskets, therefore, had to be ready for Judy to line and decorate, pack in the truck, and take off to the next show. Where the next shows that we had selected were located presented some major problems. The best shows were very often the farthest away from home and, as a consequence, traveling alone consumed a great deal of Judy's time.

Consider a typical Harvest Festival show. Often the show was in southern California and we lived in northern California. As a result of our show selection, it was necessary to do some 1,200 miles of round-trip driving. Judy would leave on Wednesday and she wouldn't be back until the following Monday. The next Wednesday or, at the latest, the next Thursday morning, she would be back on the road again, off to the next show.

It was a very grueling lifestyle, and after about five years, we just couldn't maintain it any longer. Though we were grossing a great deal of money, when we factored in expenses and time, we found that we could net just as much profit by doing some of the best shows that were closer to us. We came to a point where we passed up many great shows, in spite of our good experience with them or the fine evaluations they received in the *Crafts Fair Guide.*

Show Fees

If you noted above that we made reference to *capital outlay,* it is because the subject is especially pertinent to the problem of selecting your shows. We are not referring here to how much money you have invested in equipment and materials to produce your product, though that, of course, is also always a concern. If you don't know this or haven't considered it in depth, you must begin to do so. For it is likely that you will keep money in reserve for the production of your craft and never consider where all the money is going to come from to pay your show fees. Quite possibly, what shows you select will be drastically affected by this question.

The fees that you pay to get into a show cannot be put off and paid the morning you arrive at the show site to set up or after the show is over and you are counting your profit. At the time you mail the promoter your application, a check for her fee must be included. If your application is not accepted and you are rejected, your check will be returned to you. This means that money for perhaps dozens of shows is sitting out there somewhere in the hands of a promoter until she gets around to evaluating your application and sends you notice of acceptance or rejection.

How much money does this amount to? Well, it can easily add up to thousands of dollars. Booth fees for small neighborhood shows occasionally may cost as little as $75, but booth fees for the average show today run between $150 and $200 or more. Beth Weber's show fees for the 1999 season, included on the following pages, exemplify the typical average promotion fee. The really big show promotions cost as much as $600 for a ten-by-ten-foot booth space for three days—and each year those entry fees go up as promoters' expenses increase, just as yours do.

Beth Weber Arts & Crafts Fairs
TRUCKEE REGIONAL PARK
PO BOX 158
KINGS BEACH, CA 96143

Truckee Regional Park   <u>JURYING DEADLINE</u>
Arts and Crafts Fair   Must be received
May 27, 28, & 29   by April 25, 2000

<u>BOOTH SIZES & FEES</u>

10'x10'	(10ft frontage)	$170.00
15'x10'	(15ft frontage)	$240.00
20'x10'	(20ft frontage)	$310.00

NAME:

BUSINESS NAME:

ADDRESS:_____CITY:_____STATE:_____

ZIP:_____CA RESALE #_____PHONE :_____

Email:_____ CAR LICENSE, MAKE, STATE _____

I WILL BE SELLING:_____

_____

_____

SPACE SIZE_____

IF APPLICATION IS INCOMPLETE, IT WILL BE NOT BE JURIED

Enclosed is my NON-REFUNDABLE and NON-TRANSFERABLE, upon acceptance, entry fee, 5 PHOTOS OF MY CURRENT WORK AND 1 OF MY DISPLAY, A BUSINESS SIZE SELF ADDRESSED ENVELOPES with at least .55 postage. Please make your check payable to Beth Weber. There will be a $20 charge on all returned checks.

I agree to hold the Truckee Donner Public Utility District, and Beth Weber, harmless for any and all liability of injury and damage to life and property. By signing this application, you are agreeing that you have read and will abide by all of the rules.

SIGNATURE_____DATE:_____

What's more important to you is that the promoter wants your money early in the year and the show may not be until November or December. If you do twenty to thirty shows a year, you must have anywhere from $3,000 to $10,000 in reserve to send out before you have ever sold a dime's worth of your craft work. Even if you receive a rejection a few months after you mailed your fee and your check is returned, that money was in somebody else's possession for those few months. It was not earning anything for you. Of course, you also have no absolute guarantee—other than your past experience—that you are ever going to make this money back when you do all these shows.

Beth Weber, who has eighteen years of promoting experience, points out that the good promoter *also* has a large capital outlay, well in advance of any show she is promoting. Advertising in magazines and newspapers must be paid, street banners designed, flyers and circulars distributed, application and instruction forms printed and mailed, acceptance replies to craftspeople also mailed, salaries to staff paid, and so on.

As an example, Beth informed me that the parking lot near Kings Beach State Park at Lake Tahoe, which provides space for only seventy booths, costs $3,000 for a weekend. Therefore, the average small promoter's profit margin is not high and, over the years, costs have continually risen. In addition, fees must be paid in advance. Of the five promoters in the business whom we know best or with whom we have the most experience, only one has been extremely financially successful, while the others have simply made a modest living. Excluding the top-level shows—which are, in reality, big corporations—none of the smaller promoters have become independently wealthy.

Another Reality Check

As you contemplate and prepare for all the costs of travel to show sites, food and lodging, and all your other expenses, keep in mind that these expenses should be covered by money that you placed in reserve from your profits the previous year. Everyone who manages a crafts business successfully prepares in this way. You cannot wait and then depend on needed money being derived from earnings and profit from shows you do early in the current year. That profit, if there is much, is usually plowed back into the business and, if you have no other source of income, will be used to pay your ordinary household bills. Your goal is to sell a lot of merchandise at the best shows throughout the year. This should result in a substantial profit by the end of the year.

Once you are committed financially almost a year before the show, you had better make it to that show with a large inventory to sell. After all, you have dedicated your effort, time, and money to that weekend, well in advance, so you must be there. There is no refund on your fee should you fail to show up. The shows you select, then, depend on your having done your financial accounting well.

If you haven't gotten the picture yet, I'll reiterate that the crafts business involves a twelve- to fifteen-hour day, seven days a week, fifty-two weeks a year—and it is an expensive business in which to engage if you are doing it full-time and seriously. We don't mean to be discouraging, just realistic. On a full-time basis, you must be prepared to eat, sleep, and even dream about the business, and how and what shows you select is a major part of that business and those dreams.

Your lifestyle will have a carnival or circus atmosphere. Many people believe that craftspeople travel from show to show as a group. There will be times when your business will seem to pervade your daily existence and exclude what most people consider a normal life. Many of our previous friendships were lost because we were simply never available, as we once had been. If we were not so busy in the production of our craft, we were busy planning for the next season. We can't count the family get-togethers we missed, the parties we couldn't attend, the places we couldn't go.

If you're not the kind of person who can adjust to this gypsy style of life and the pressure it creates, don't attempt to go into this business full-time—especially your first year or two. Get your feet good and wet before you decide to make that kind of commitment. What we've just said may be the best reason of all for making your show selections carefully. It's hell to be sitting at a rotten show, knowing you missed a friend's wedding or a relative's birthday or anniversary.

Some General Advice

If you are just starting out, keep your travel expenses to a minimum. If possible, put your money in your product and only venture as far away as is absolutely necessary. But don't stick around the neighborhood, as we did. Apply to good shows! Certainly, don't select some local, Sunday in the park show just because it is nearby. A few hundred neighbors won't help you honestly evaluate your product or your sales ability. At good shows, your entry fees will be higher, but so will the attendance. The result is that you will get a truer picture of the marketability of your product.

In summing up this chapter, we would say that in your novice years, your show selection should probably include a smattering of all the types of shows we have discussed, whether you applied to them originally by recommendation, gamble, or research. Little by little, you will discard the failures and reapply to the shows that were successful for *you*, not successful for someone who told you how great it was "last year." Slowly, you will build an annual schedule that you approach each year with confidence and anticipation. Then you will also come to know the special excitement and sense of accomplishment that comes with the unexpected success and the even greater sense of achievement when you know you have planned your craft season well.

6

The Promoter

*I*F NOTHING THAT WE HAVE SAID HAS DISCOURAGED YOU thus far—and we hope it hasn't—we now will deal with the people who may have more to do with the success of your business, in some ways, than even you yourself. As confident as you now may be that you have a unique and beautiful product—one to which the buying public will respond enthusiastically—without the promoter, the person who produces the craft shows in which you desire to showcase your craft, essentially you have no business. You are completely dependent on the promoter.

Though you may be convinced that you and your product are ready to meet the world of customers who will spend a great deal of money purchasing your craft, you have nowhere to set up your booth and ply your trade until you can convince the promoter of that. So, having considered all the advice you have been given (including ours), having scoured the craft fair guides and decided on the shows that you think are best suited to selling your product, now, all you have to do is apply to those shows, show up on the specified date, and sell. Right? Wrong!

The Process of Applying

As we noted briefly in the previous chapter, whether you are new to the business or one of the thousands of veteran artisans, long established in the Big Time craft arena, if you are applying to shows that you have never done before, you will first have to mail your request for an application to each promoter of every craft show you have selected. While you are waiting for a response, this is a good time to initiate a filing system regarding promoters and their promotions.

Make a list of every show for which you requested an application, the date and place of that show, the deadline for applying to the show, and the date you mailed your request. Then check it off when you receive the application back in the mail. That way you don't lose track of the shows to which you have already applied. This is easy to do when you are sending out many such requests. Then be sure to request applications for many more shows than you intend to do. If you want to participate in twenty shows in a given year, send out requests for applications to twenty-five, as you can expect to receive some rejections no matter how long you have been in the business.

It is not at all unusual for a few weeks to pass, sometimes more, before the application you requested arrives in your mailbox. So while you are anxiously waiting, just keep producing your product. Even though you're spending more time and money at this point, and you have no idea whether you will ever be accepted when you do finally apply, that's just another gamble of the business.

If it's any consolation, once you are in the business and have established yourself, you'll be getting applications and invitations automatically. If you're good, almost all doors will be open to you—more shows than you could possibly do. Don't just throw those applications and invitations out. File them away. Next year you may want them.

Whether you're new to the business or a veteran, whether the application was sent to you automatically or you had to request it, when you have the application in hand, it is not just a simple matter of filling it out, attaching a check, and sending it right back to the promoter with the expectation that you will be admitted to the show. A laborious process called *jurying* begins and, no matter how long you are in the business, you will go through this every time you apply to a new show or one staged by a new promoter. Some shows still require you to be juried every year, even if you have been accepted to them before. You will also be required to jury again if you have added any new products to your craft line.

Promoters and the Jury System

To *jury* your craft is the process by which you convince each promoter that you manufacture a product and can present a booth display that he wants to accept into his show. Promoters are always looking for new products to give their show variety and booth displays that repeat customers have not seen before. There could be 300 to 500 craft booths in the top shows like Harvest Festival or Country Folk Art. Most of the artisans will be among the very best from all over the country, and the jury system is the reason why.

The best promoters are very careful, selective, and discriminating in this regard, as they should be, for your sake as well as theirs. The average promoter depends on booth fees to defray all the cost of promotion and still render a profit. The larger promoters depend on admission fees to cover the expenses that booth fees do not, and to produce the necessary profit to remain in business. It is in both their interests and yours to provide the public with a display of crafts that intrigue them and keep them returning to the show, year after year. Rhonda Blakely expressed Country Folk Arts' philosophy as follows: "trying to present to the customer a total decorating theme."

This dedication to giving the customers their money's worth is especially true of promotions that charge what seem like especially high booth fees. Such shows as Harvest Festival and Country Folk Art travel nationwide. For years, Country Folk Art had its own magazine with 75,000 subscribers and a circulation of half a million. Yet, as costs of producing the magazine doubled, the publication had to be discontinued. Harvest Festival maintains its own Web site. Obviously, these big promotions have long-standing reputations for quality to maintain, even as they struggle with the same increasing business costs as you do, only on a much larger scale.

Many craftspeople may not believe it—even though it is true—but as one promoter assured me, "Promoters respect their exhibitors and want to help them to continue to be successful." And this is the attitude of good promoters everywhere, for the relationship between craftsperson and promoter is a symbiotic one. Both need each other to be successful and to make a profit. Another promoter put it this way: "I understand their concerns regarding increased expenses, but in order to maintain the level of promotion we all want, we need to stay on top of the markets, and advertise and upgrade our shows as much as we can each season." To do that costs big money. In some markets, Rhonda Blakely informed me, radio advertising now costs as much as television commercials, and the cost of print advertising has doubled.

Other large shows, like the Garlic Festival in California, a once-a-year community endeavor that draws 100,000 people, does not have the substantial budget of corporate promotions. The manager and workers all volunteer their time, and profits from admissions fees are all earmarked for various community projects. As a daytime show, it requires no lights (no electrical bill), and since it is a well-established, well-known show, there is no need for promotion beyond the flyers they send out to craftspeople and local TV and radio to notify them of the date. The entry fee is far less than that charged by big corporate shows with huge budgets to support.

If your application to the Garlic Festival is accepted, you are going to make a bundle of money that one weekend. Just don't count on being accepted. Such annuals as this usually allow no more than eighty to a hundred crafters in the show, primarily to maintain their tradition. These types of traditional shows usually have a nucleus of artists who have shown with them for years, many since the inaugural presentation. Participants often live in the local community and are invited back every year. So they may only accept some fifteen or twenty new craftspeople into their show each year and receive as many as five hundred applications for those few spots. Do not be dismayed if you are not accepted. As profitable as they can be, you should never rely on them as a year-to-year source of income.

We want to advise you, too, that with smaller shows, a promoter may reject you, not because of the quality of your craft, but because he may have already accepted into the show a few craftspeople producing pieces similar to yours. Therefore, there are even fewer booth spaces open to you, no matter how fine your product. So, after a few years of applying to and being rejected by these shows, you may decide it is pointless to keep applying—particularly if there is a nonrefundable jury fee—whether you are accepted to the show or not. More than a few promotions derive considerable extra profit through this fee.

Whether the promotion is of the average size or one of the big shows, they would quickly stop drawing huge crowds of customers, willing to pay admission year after year, if they were not providing the public with a large variety of well-produced crafts. To jury for the vast, top-of-the-line promotions is, therefore, the most difficult, particularly for those of you just entering the business.

What good promoters are looking for can be stated in very simple terms. As Judy and I recognized early in our career, and as described by every promoter I've interviewed, their standards are the same. Promoters seek, quality and skill. They examine the raw material that goes into the product, design originality, how the product is embellished that distinguishes it from another craftsperson's similar product, and artistic design. Achieve that and you'll probably be accepted.

Now, of course, as in any other business, there will be those promoters who don't discriminate at all. Just send in your application and if they are not already filled, you're in. As you progress in the craft world and encounter the various promoters, you will find that this is not the attitude of the best promoters or even the majority.

Some promoters really care about craftspeople. Beth Weber, who only promotes shows in the north Lake Tahoe area, is a good example. She sees them as *artisans*. She is herself a potter and exhibits at every show she promotes. She acknowledges that "Some promoters forget why they are making their money." Beth is discriminating in the craftspeople she selects for her shows and appreciative of each artisan's contribution to the success of her shows.

Unfortunately, Beth is not representative of every promoter you will encounter. You will experience disappointment with shows that operate on that nondiscriminating basis. And you will get to know which promoters are concerned only with the money they make. Yet, there will be times that, in spite of this knowledge, you won't be able to avoid doing their shows. Some craft shows, when put on by even the least likable promoters, must be given your consideration because they will make you money!

These are the street fairs that include as many as 500 to 800 other craft booths. These really large street shows are often promoted by people long in the business, contracted year after year to promote the same show. Other than mailing out acceptances, marking booth spaces, and collecting money, they do little real promoting. Every organization in the community is really promoting the show for the promoter, months in advance of the show date. The show draws such huge crowds, representing every economic segment of the population, that the promoter does not have to be at all discerning or discriminating with regard to the quality of crafts presented at the show. These promoters will accept every conceivable kind of craft and quality level of craft, until they have no more booth spaces to fill. It's not that the jurying is lax; it's just that even though photographs of your work will be requested, jurying is really nonexistent. Do not regard your acceptance to this type of show as a recognition of your work. However, this is one of the rare times that it doesn't matter. Your craft will be seen by thousands of people who are interested in the market that your craft represents and exposure is the name of the game.

Handling a Rejection

Many times, regardless of how long you have been in the business and even in seemingly indiscriminate situations such as the above example, you will be rejected, and you will never know exactly why. If a promoter puts on many shows a year, you may be rejected for some and accepted into others. That can be hard to understand. When you are rejected, it is worth your effort to write a courteous letter requesting an explanation from the promoter. Doing so demonstrates your interest, concern, and professionalism. Just the fact that the promoter responds and perhaps gives you a few tips suggests that you have a good chance to get into next year's show or shows, assuming you address the reason you were rejected. Remember, your livelihood depends on the promoter's decision, so it always behooves you to put your best, most genial, and professional foot forward.

The Process of Jurying

There are basically two forms or ways to jury. The first is the submission of photographs of your craft and booth display along with your application and a check for your jurying fee. The second is the in-person jury process. In this case, you will be given a time and place to appear, and you must present your craft to one or more people—on occasion, a whole committee—for their evaluation and approval. Sometimes, they will tell you immediately whether or not you have been accepted and, if not, why not.

This in-person jurying process can be extremely helpful to you, but other times, you will just place your craft product on display with many other products, be told when to return to retrieve your merchandise, and be sent your acceptance or rejection in the mail. This form of jurying is less common; most often, you just submit photographs or slides. And the mail-submission process is certainly a more convenient way of presenting your craft to the promoter.

However, while in-person jurying may be very inconvenient—since you will have to take time out from the production of your craft to travel to wherever the jury process is taking place—it is to your best advantage and very much worth the expenditure of your time. If you receive comments about your craft—verbally or in writing—positive feedback will tell you what you are doing right and negative appraisal will tell you what you need to improve.

Granted, a rejection based on putting your craft on the line before this type of jury can be ego-shattering and very demoralizing. But, whatever the outcome, this type of jury procedure is an excellent learning experience for you, as it is the most honest critique you will probably ever receive regarding your craft. Friends and neighbors are usually not going to tell you the truth, simply because they don't want to hurt your feelings.

The in-person jury offers a practical, realistic, professional appraisal of your work that can give you a perspective that you never considered, one which you may find very useful as you develop your product line. Remember that even when you jury in-person, since you cannot set up your booth for them, the jury will expect to see photographs of your booth display. We will give you more details regarding photographs later in this chapter.

While to jury in this manner presents a good opportunity to have your product evaluated, it also does not mean that every promoter, jury, or committee will evaluate your product the same way. What does not fulfill the needs of one promoter may be exactly to the liking of another. Your product may be excellent, but too similar to other crafts already accepted into the show. Most good promoters try not to have more than two or three of the same category in a normal-size show. Another promoter might not have anything like your work in his show. Then, too, the size of one show may be more limited than another.

Country Folk Art and Harvest Festival both try very hard to find artisans who produce everything themselves, which tells you something about the concerns of these promoters. However, they both acknowledge that maintaining that approach is becoming more difficult. The handmade crafts coming from overseas are not only increasing in quantity, but also improving in quality. Furthermore, customers who once wanted to buy only American are beginning to change their philosophy if the foreign product is good and is of course, less expensive. Then, too, some labor-intensive products are now almost entirely relegated to foreign craftspeople. Rhonda Blakely gave me the example of lace or tatted goods. It is now virtually impossible to find anyone who produces this type of product in the United States. All this creates stiffer competition.

Yet another problem that you may encounter relates to specific crafts. Some promoters will not accept certain kinds of product in their shows—ceramics, for example—as they do not consider a product that comes out of a mold original, no matter how well it is cast and how superb the artistic embellishments. Other promoters specialize in fine arts only, so if your craft is not in that category, you are wasting your time applying. Read the promoter's specifications carefully. And once you are accepted through this process, it should give you new confidence in what you are selling and how you are displaying it.

As mentioned above, to jury by photo is the most common practice and the most convenient. The promoter will want, not only photos or slides of your product, but photos of your booth display as well. Several excellent examples of beautiful, intriguing, and inviting booths are included in the chapter on Booth Setup and Booth Display, where this subject is discussed in extensive detail. For now, be advised only that if you find yourself applying to shows that do not require such photos, you certainly can apply as a beginner just for the experience but, for the most part, forget the show. This promoter is not too interested in the quality of the show or the quality of your work and so you are apt to find yourself in a flea market environment. Such shows usually don't last year after year, as customers today are far more sophisticated than they were years ago. Many enthusiastic, regular attendees of craft shows will show up at a show site, scan it quickly, get back into their car, and go to another show. They will not return the following year.

Photographing Your Craft and Your Booth Display

Throughout our years in the business, I can only guess that Judy and I must have taken hundreds and hundreds of pictures of every kind of basket we created. We took them outdoors and indoors, in sunlight and in shade, from every angle possible and ended up throwing away most of them and wasting a lot of time and money.

The object, as you'd expect, is to take photos that show your product line to its best advantage. Colors should be vivid and size should be obvious. The use to which the craft may be put should be demonstrated; that is, dolls on a bed or in a cradle, shelves on a wall, a sewing basket next to a rocking chair, pottery on a table, rings on a finger, and so on. That certainly seems simple enough—if you are a decent photographer. We couldn't believe how difficult taking a simple photograph of our product turned out to be. Hadn't I taken a thousand great pictures of the kids? You bet! Most likely, so have you! Now, think about how many rotten pictures of the children and the family, and the dog you've thrown away. If your answer is the same as ours, unless you are an excellent photographer and have a good camera, hire a professional. This advice comes not just from us, but from promoters like Beth Weber who told us about the many craftspeople she had to reject throughout the years because the photographs they sent in were poor examples of their work. She added, "If I only had one space and two people's craft work were of equal quality, then the photograph of the booth would define who was accepted." Assuming that both the craft workmanship and the photographs were of equal quality, another promoter told me that the craftsperson's reputation would become the deciding factor. Obviously, if you are a beginner, you have no reputation, so the photographs are all you can rely on to make a good impression.

Judy and I will never know how many rejections we received because of the quality of our photographs. Promoters often told us, when we were finally accepted to their shows, "If I had known how beautiful your work was, I would have accepted you last year." We were told that our photographs lacked clarity and the rich color of the fabrics used in our baskets didn't look true. When we then compared our original pictures with the photographs taken by a professional, we quickly realized that the angle of our pictures was wrong or the colors were washed out. In some cases, the setting in which we placed the basket was more prominent in the picture than the basket itself. In others, the background was wrong or the lighting insufficient or too intense. I'd guess that for every picture that came out well, we threw six or seven away, maybe more. We had better luck photographing our booth display. Even in shooting the booth, sometimes we were too far away and sometimes too close, or the interior was too dark or too light.

Certain crafts magnify the photographic problem even more. Jewelry is an especially good example of a product that is most difficult to photograph. The problems of lighting and particularly reflection misrepresenting and distorting the image are immensely difficult for the amateur photographer to overcome. We wasted $500 on a very good camera and still made mistakes.

It must be said honestly that we've also seen extremely poor photography work by more than one professional, but by and large, it is a lot less expensive in the long run to hire a professional photographer, even though the initial cost is substantial. It is basically a one-time expense until you add new products to your line. Just have enough copies made, select the best carefully, and keep the negatives. Then you are ready to send every promoter as many photographs as is required. Those photographs will be returned to you if your application is rejected and, if accepted, the promoter usually returns them at the show. Just remember that photographs are an expense on which you cannot afford to try to save money. The photograph, in most instances, is all that there is to represent you and your work, and the only way the promoter can fully appreciate the quality of that work.

One promoter also pointed out to me that a photograph can also be used to *misrepresent* the craftsperson's work. It is not uncommon for some craftspeople to send in photographs of one craft item, on which basis they are accepted to the show, and then display numerous other kinds of merchandise that were not juried and that would not have been accepted. Some promoters, for example, will not allow any product that has been manufactured out of the country. For that matter, many customers will leave a show without making a purchase if they observe too many crafts manufactured in foreign countries. If you're discovered doing this, you may be asked to leave the show or the promoter will reject your application to any future shows.

Acceptance or Rejection Can Be in the Details

We have discussed the jury process and complaints about it with any number of craftsman and promoters over the years. We came to realize that, in most instances, the reason for rejections was often failure to do a few simple things. So we'd like to pass these simple tips along to you.

When discussing show selection, most of the craftspeople we met would tell us that they just filled out the application form, enclosed a few pictures, and mailed the package in. At first, we took that same approach and got routine results, meaning we received some acceptances and some rejections. Then we changed our approach and rarely were rejected thereafter, as long as our application was submitted on time. Here's what we did, and what we suggest that you do.

When submitting photos of your product and booth fully set up, enclose a letter about yourself. Write the letter in a general manner that can pertain to every show to which you will apply, so that you are not rewriting the entire letter every time you apply to a show. Write the letter in such a way as to introduce yourself to the promoter, portraying who you are as an individual. To save time, put the letter on your computer, so that, thereafter, you only have to change the names and addresses of the promoters.

Another way to look at it is to use the letter as a vehicle to promote yourself and your craft. Sell yourself! Tell the promoter about your business history and the quality of products used in the manufacturing of your craft. Include background on your training, expertise, or qualifications in the field and any awards you've received from other promoters.

If you use a mailing list, mention that, too, and explain the extent of your customer following. This is important to the promoter because it means more people will attend the show and, if there is an admission charge, more money will end up in the promoter's pocket. Rich Burleigh informed me that "Many promoters depend a great deal on attendance generated by the mailing lists of applicants to their shows." If you have a store, include that information, and if you've had any press coverage, attach the press clips. This letter or resume sets you apart in the mind of the promoter. Just as name recognition is important in the corporate world, it has its place in the craft world as well.

Nevertheless, you may still receive a rejection letter. If you request an explanation by letter, some promoters will respond to your letter and others will not. The promoters who answer do so because they are impressed with your sincerity, your professionalism, and your obvious interest in their shows. Since their income depends on craftspeople who are willing to pay a substantial fee to enter their shows, if they are really fully professional in the way they run their business, they will find some time to answer your letter. If they do not respond, usually because of a busy schedule, they will generally file the letter away and will probably refer to it and remember you next year, if you apply again. In fact, remind them of the letter or send another, updated letter when you apply next year.

If a show you are considering applying to is in your locale, and you have a free day, go to it, evaluate it, and introduce yourself to the promoter—when she is not frantically busy. Try to meet the promoter after you have walked the entire show, talked to other craftspeople, and appraised customer attendance and buying response. When you find the promoter, if you still want to apply to the show, you have something to talk to her about. Perhaps you can pay the promoter some compliment on the show. If your application to the show was rejected, you can express your disappointment and say how much you are hoping to be accepted next year. Probably, she won't remember your application or why it was rejected, but next year, you'll have a better chance of being remembered. The promoter will have a face and a personality to put to the name when going through a stack of applications. Include a picture of yourself outside your booth just to further refresh the promoter's memory. In your letter, remind her of your on-site meeting.

Before we leave the subject of promoters, you should be aware that, as a group, the good promoters all agree that there are certain rules they set for their shows, about which they are very strict and which they will enforce. Their rules can sometimes seem very annoying, vexing, arbitrary, and trivial, and the promoter knows they are viewed this way. But, like them or not, it is most important that you adhere to them.

When you are accepted to a promoter's show, in your acceptance packet you will receive all the rules pertaining to the show. In some cases, the rules will include the time you are scheduled to arrive and unload your vehicle. Try to be punctual in this regard, as the rule is made because there are not enough unloading areas to allow every vehicle to arrive at the same time. Arrive at the wrong time and you may have to wait hours to unload and set up, and you may not complete the job before the show opens. You also may irritate the promoter who is trying to manage the parking problem and facilitate unloading. Two other rules that almost all promoters make and enforce relate to closing time and when you may begin to break down your booth and bring in your vehicle for loading.

If you are tempted to tear down your booth early, just because the crowd is thinning out and you doubt that you will have any more customers, don't do it. Whether they arrived late to the show or not—and especially if they paid to get in—all customers have the right to expect to see every booth in place and you prepared to sell to them. Should the promoter catch you violating this rule, you may get nothing but a warning or you may not be accepted to any of the promoter's future shows.

You will also be instructed as to where to park your vehicle after you have unloaded it. Usually, you are to park it there throughout the entire show. You can expect that this will be somewhat inconvenient, as sometimes it may be blocks away from the show site. However, there is a very good reason for this: The show is there to serve the customer, not you as the merchant. To whatever extent possible, the rule is there to provide the customers with easy parking and easy access to their vehicles. Oftentimes, purchases can be taken to a vehicle parked close by rather than be carried around all day. This convenience could make the difference in a sale to you and is in your best interests. Customers who cannot park or cannot walk long distances to their cars are not going to stop at the show and they are not going to buy from you. Elderly people and the handicapped need easy access to the show site. They cannot and will not walk blocks and blocks to the show. Just walking the show may be difficult enough.

If you are caught violating this rule, you can again be sure that you will not be invited back by the promoter. Beth Weber told us that getting craftspeople to obey the rules she sets is probably one of the biggest problems that she and every promoter has. When rule violation is flagrant, she and most other promoters will ask the craftsperson to pack up and leave. As Beth sees it, "The rules are made to serve the customers and therefore benefit you." As in every other aspect of life, promoters cannot be lumped together or stereotyped. It would be wonderful if all promoters were like those quoted thus far. Unfortunately, that is not life. They run the gamut from consummate professionals to absolute sleezeballs. You will like some and despise others. Some promoters you will get to know personally and together celebrate your mutual triumphs. Others you will never meet at all, and still others you will want to stay as far away from as possible—even after you are accepted to their show.

In fact, in some shows, it is not the promoter who juries the applications but a committee you will never know or see. A promoter may have been hired simply to handle publicity and to offer name recognition to those submitting their applications. The committee itself may change its composition from year to year. Consequently, the committee who loved your work one year may be supplanted by another to whom your work does not appeal at all.

We were accepted to a state college campus eight years in a row, while friends with quality crafts would be accepted one year, rejected for the next two years, then be accepted again. When this happens, it can be very devastating to your projected financial expectations for the year. Since you had not anticipated a rejection, you may have to fill in with another show. In this instance, it was just a matter of the personal taste of those students comprising the committee. Still another unknown factor in the crafts business. You gamble and you have to accept the results.

Virtually all promoters send you your booth assignment number with your acceptance letter. Big shows may even send you a diagram of the show site from which you may select your spot. A sample diagram can be seen on the opposite page. My least favorite promoter, however, is one of the few who will not provide you with your booth space in advance. This promoter will also punish you if you don't apply to enough of his shows, keeping you out of his best shows or assigning you an undesirable space.

Here's the way he "planned" some of the events we participated in. On the show date, every craftsperson arrived at 5 A.M. and stood in the dark while names were called, as if we were all in the Army. Next we were each handed space assignments in a sealed envelope, as if it were a military secret. Then, 700 or more craftspeople scrambled to find their assigned spaces in order to set up on time, in a show that covered many city avenues and side streets. They ran to their vehicles, a la Le Mans, and engaged in a road race that resembled the beginning of a Demolition Derby.

It was a terribly stressful way to begin the day. Thereafter, this promoter was never seen until it was time to pay him his percentage fees at the end of the show. However, this promoter's shows attracted crowds of over 100,000 people each day and, even competing against some 700 other craftspeople, we always made a lot of money. This was the show's saving grace, the bottom line. The bottom line is the reason you are there.

The Percentage Show

If you are new to this entire procedure and the craft world, you may not be aware that some shows ask not only a booth fee, but also 10–15 percent of your gross. A lot of cheating goes on with regard to this percentage, as no promoter can monitor the sales taking place in every booth. Basically, a perverted honor system prevails. The truth is that very few craftspeople we knew really paid an honest percentage to the promoter. And the promoter knows, and probably even expects, this.

Some people rationalize ways to pay less, considering it fair to subtract all their expenses from their gross earnings and then pay the promoter's percentage on what remains. They usually express the opinion that the promoter did not earn it in the first place. This may be, but it is beside the point. You knew it was a percentage show when you applied. Others will just not pay it at all, but they

DIRECTIONS:
I-15 East or West, merge onto Hwy 95 going South
Take L.V. Blvd/Cashman Field exit
Turn left on Las Vegas Blvd.

North on 95
Take downtown exit
Turn right Las Vegas Blvd.
Entrances to Cashman Field are right off Las Vegas Blvd.

LAS VEGAS
AUGUST 27-28-29

Cashman Center
850 Las Vegas Blvd. North
Las Vegas, NV 89109
702-386-7100 Fax: 702-386-7126

EXHIBITOR MOVE-IN
Enter off Las Vegas Blvd. at Lot A or East
Washington at Lot C.

No charge for parking on move-in day until
5pm, after which parking cost is $2.00.

*Subject to change.
 Always check onsite with show personnel

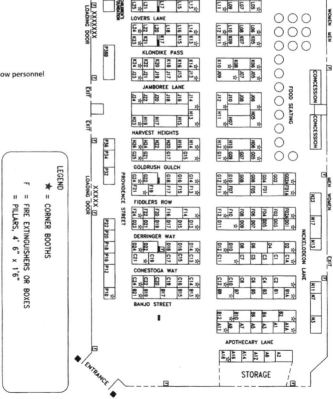

can expect a letter from the promoter, as one does sign a contractual agreement to pay that percentage. Do this once, and even if you get away with it, you will never be accepted to that show again. Still others will pay the promoter a larger percentage than they really earned, just to ensure their acceptance into next year's show or to ensure a better booth space the following year. Another craftsperson won't want his actual take "on the record," thereby hiding his true earnings from Uncle Sam.

The upshot of all this is that what you read in a *Crafts Fair Guide* may not be a reflection of what the craftsperson really earned and, perhaps, since money earned is a measure of the shows you select, not a fair way to always evaluate the promoter of those shows or the show itself. Sometimes you just have to do the show to find out for yourself.

Frankly, I've always wished that promoters would simply charge a higher entry fee and do away with the percentage since so much skullduggery goes on. We tried to avoid commission shows when possible, but don't rule them out completely when making your selections. Caution! It *will* hurt when you do a $4,000 gross show and have to write out a check to the promoter for $400.

Happily, promoters who engage in the negative practices we have described are relatively rare. As detestable as some types of promoters may or may not be to you, if their shows create an arena in which you are financially successful, both our and your personal opinion is irrelevant. It should never affect your decision to do a show—unless you have been accepted to a better show. Since exposure serves your ends best, the more the better, you sometimes can't be too choosy.

Unfortunately, promoters like Beth Weber and Rich Burleigh, who seek to help the individual craftspeople, are becoming more and more rare. According to Beth, "Some promoters seem to be more interested in the money to be made, than their interrelationship with the craftspeople who apply to their shows." In the future, that may become part of the reality with which you must learn to live.

One of the nicest promoters, a woman whose shows were called Lady Bug Boutique, helped us a great deal in our early years. Eventually, she went out of business. Saturation of the area by the bigger shows simply took away her customer base. We regretted no longer applying to her shows, but as the show attracted fewer and fewer people, we had no choice. That is the nature of all business, no different than what happened to the mom-and-pop grocery store as supermarkets proliferated. Much of the personal touch was lost.

Remember Your Monetary Goal

Particularly when you're starting out in the business, you must simply ignore your personal likes and dislikes. You must learn to live with your decision for the weekend. You paid money for the privilege, so only what you walk away with at the end of the weekend, really counts—unless you are independently wealthy. But, then, why are you doing craft shows at all?

It is nice to apply to and be accepted into shows where the promoters come around from one booth to another, introduce themselves, ask if you need anything, listen patiently to your complaints, try to correct them, and demonstrate sensitive concern about your needs, even inquiring as to whether you are happy and having a successful show. But that is rare. If you are looking for that, you're in the wrong world.

Some promoters like Beth Weber actually do this and have coffee and doughnuts for everybody while they are setting up. But you cannot expect or anticipate this. Just enjoy it when it happens—but bring your own coffee and doughnuts most of the time.

When you are an established success, you can be more selective about promoters, but don't bank on it even then. As an artisan selling your wares, you must always search for new shows, never knowing what you'll encounter. Some of the nicest promoters we knew promoted some of the least profitable shows and vice versa.

All you have to do to evaluate the potential of a show is to observe the extent of television and newspaper advertising devoted to it, and whether there are banners and posters around the town and hung throughout the area well in advance of the show. If that was done properly, then the resulting attendance is the only major factor of concern to you. If the crowds come out, the rest is up to you.

Promotional Costs Are Rising

Since so many craftspeople complain about the increasing cost of booth space from one year to the next, this is a good point to give you some idea of the increasing cost to the promoter. While these figures will not apply to every show to which you are accepted, they represent an accurate account of the top promotions and may not be far off for the average promoter who does a conscientious job of advertising.

I queried Harvest Festival, in business now for twenty-seven years, concerning the extent to which their cost of operation has gone up over the years. They indicated that the cost of advertising has gone up roughly 10–15 percent, and the cost of renting facilities in which to present their shows has risen 10–12 percent. That does not take into consideration the continually increasing cost of general overhead, and the cost of doing business—things like staff salaries, travel expenses, decorations, and much more. In fact, all the booth fees combined pay only 65 percent of the media advertising expense.

Escalating costs have, therefore, substantially impacted the crafts business. Just being able to rent the best facilities on the best dates is also becoming a significant problem. There is increasing competition with trade shows and conventions that bring in more people to an area and so acquire priority status. Obviously, then, if promoters of these top shows are to make the profit that they deserve, it must be derived from the number of people they can attract to the show who are willing to pay an admission fee.

Considering those factors, the individual craftsperson should recognize that if the show draws large crowds, the promoter has done his job. You can ask no more! The rest is up to you. Therefore, perhaps this is the proper place to discuss all the reasons, alibis, and excuses that even professionals, long in the business, will use to explain their failure to make money.

Excuses, Alibis, and Blaming the Promoter

Having selected a show and having been accepted, it is best that you learn to accept the conditions under which you are doing business. Then learn from experience and evaluate the show to determine whether you will apply again next year, or make another selection for that particular weekend. Do your own quiet analysis and try to come to your own conclusions. This is made difficult by other craftspeople, who can affect your judgment and prejudice your evaluation.

During a show, you will socialize and discuss the status of the show with many of your neighbors. You will see their booth activity and they will see yours. When those in the crafts business are not selling, many will seek any explanation that they can conjure up. They will imagine and explore every avenue of excuse except that theirs is a poor product or one that does not sell in that marketplace.

Craftspeople will blame the miserable heat, extreme cold, the wind and rain, the economy, lack of customer taste, lousy promotion, and even the fact that it is Sunday and everyone is going to church. Heat, cold, rain, and snow may be valid reasons for poor attendance or apathetic buying but, if the people are there, it means the promoter did his job in getting them to the show site in spite of the weather or any other conditions. Given that, you should be getting your share of the business or something is wrong with *you!*

Many, many times, we had some of our best shows under the worst conditions. More than once, rain or the threat of rain led to a buying frenzy. If a show was good last year, you shouldn't, under most circumstances, let the weather in the area affect your decision to select that show. One of the biggest annual craft shows is in a little town in Nevada. It has a seventy-five-year history and, though it may well snow, you don't bypass this show. We never grossed less than $5,000 during the two-day run of this show, no matter what the weather conditions.

You also don't select shows because they are set in a pretty park or because you can take a swim in the lake or because they have eternal sunshine. Rating the general environment in which a show takes place and how certain conditions may affect sales is legitimate. But, if the crowds are there, the environment cannot be used as an excuse. If many people did go to church, because it happens to be a particularly Godly community, that never stops them from coming out and spending twice as much in the afternoon—if you have what they want to buy. Look to yourself and your product. Don't blame the promoter if the people are there.

Another excuse you will hear frequently relates to the vendors who are your immediate neighbors. On rare occasions, this can be a problem; for example, you may be assigned a space next to a noisy booth, selling raucous music. It may be annoying, but it probably isn't the reason for your lack of sales. The promoter has to put *somebody* next to that booth. You have to learn to live with these situations. Some shows and some booths are just plain noisier than others, especially at street fairs with rock-and-roll bands. You are going to set up next to all kinds of people, and you may be stuck right near a bandstand.

For years we did a show where our regular booth space was right in front of the stage, and we listened to blaring country western music for three days. To be heard, we had to practically scream at the customers and they to us. That never stopped us from selecting that show and we never asked Rich Burleigh to change our booth space.

Rich, who runs a promotion called Fire on the Mountain, is one of the better small promoters here in California. I say small only because he and his wife only promote three or four shows each year. But those shows are big, traditional events with twenty or more years of history behind them. They draw extremely large crowds; have wonderful, varied, and free entertainment; and keep people at the show all day. If you can't sell and make a profit at Rich's shows, you can't make money anywhere.

Rich was doing us a favor giving us that space I mentioned. He had three buildings filled with crafts and he moved us progressively into the best building and gave us one of the best booth spaces. Everybody with any experience wanted that space. When the bands were playing and the entertainment was taking place, crowds of people stood in front of our booth, the length of the building to watch—and everybody was looking right at our booth when they did so. Sure, we didn't do much business while the band was playing a set, but we did three times as much when the set was over.

Only a very few shows send you the layout of the show and give you an advance choice as to space location. Most often you have to be long established with these shows to be given such choice. Try to be happy that you were accepted and realize that your space is the luck of the draw. Try to make it work to your advantage. Often, having the most disreputable-looking booth next to you is a plus. If you have a beautiful booth, you look superbly professional and artistic by comparison.

We were once assigned a space next to a vendor selling children's swings. Another time, it was an ice cream stand. In both cases, mothers didn't want to wait on line or stand there while their children swung back and forth for an hour. Both booths became a noisy babysitter, while the mothers shopped in our booth. Sure, kids came looking for their mother and one or two dropped ice cream in a basket, but it was worth it. Since all our fabrics were Scotch-guarded, they wiped clean easily and if they were soiled we relined the baskets.

The same principle applies should the booth next to you have a similar product. If your product is better, you stand out by comparison, whereas, had the similar product been two aisles away, the customer might have already made a purchase there before ever seeing what you have to sell. Promoters frequently are castigated for this and they needn't be. We always found that when it happened, we benefited. The customer has an obvious choice. If they choose to make a purchase from your competitor next door, put aside your ego, objectively evaluate your competition, and try to determine what it is about the competitor's craft work that the customer found superior to yours. Learn from every experience of this kind.

In none of these instances should you make an excuse for yourself by blaming the promoter and then next year allow it to affect your show selection. While promoters should and usually do try to stagger booths with similar crafts, mistakes can happen. Think positive and make the best of the situation. Next year, you'll be given a different space. If, when you apply the following year, you are absolutely convinced that booth placement caused you a serious problem, explain that in a letter to the promoter and, very often, the mistake will be rectified. Most promoters try to be as accommodating as possible.

Occasionally, you'll run into a problem we touched on earlier—one that is more difficult to assess. Say, every craftsperson with whom you talk has had a successful show, but you've done poorly. You are convinced it is not related to the quality of your product or how well the show was promoted. What is wrong may be the connection between your product and the local market, as in the following scenario.

Our baskets were considered country traditional and so they were simply not a product that would sell well at a San Francisco street show where mostly local citizenry were in attendance. Just thirty miles away on the peninsula, or across the Golden Gate Bridge, we were in sync with the local market. We learned our lesson and thereafter applied to only one show in San Francisco, a big show held in the convention center that drew customers from all over the Bay Area.

When this kind of situation occurs, we did not make excuses for ourselves and our lack of sales. We evaluated the problem in an objective, businesslike manner. It is much like sending a story to a publisher. It is your responsibility to research publishers. Choose the wrong publisher and you receive a rejection, no matter how good your material. Remember! It is your responsibility to research the craft shows that you select and to which you apply. The promoter may like your work very much and just be seeking diversity in the show. The promoter cannot guarantee your marketability.

Be Careful about These Promotions

There are a number of other types of promotions and promoters that fall into special categories and do deserve special attention. Every craftsperson has been lured into these shows at least once, primarily because the promoter does not require you to jury—and could care less about quality. To many in the business, old or new, this kind of show can offer a new experience, a new world, and new opportunity. When you've received a bunch of rejections and need immediate income, it is easy to apply to and select one of these types of shows, and to fall into the trap. We fell into the trap after fifteen years in the business, simply because we had a free weekend, our inventory was well stocked, and I convinced Judy to gamble a little. I got greedy and greed can be another trap.

Generally, these shows fall into broad categories: carnival/rodeo promotions, food and gift shows, antique car or antique furniture shows, rod and gun shows, rib or chili or whatever cook-offs, and shows put on by specific private clubs and social organizations. With the exception of shows run by private clubs and organizations, the others all present the same problems and you should generally avoid selecting any of them unless you are financially desperate and in need of picking up even small change, or unless you sell an item like T-shirts that you can adapt to the specific groups of people who attend these shows. Belts and belt buckles and dime-store jewelry may move also, but that's about it.

The reason to avoid these shows is that the promoter is not really interested in quality crafts. Nor is the promoter's reputation based on crafts promotion. This promoter basically puts on big events, often being sponsored by the town who hires the promoter. It may even be a traditional event.

Whatever the case, a big event is being promoted and crafts are merely an addendum, an extra added attraction, often spaced far from the main event, area, or arena where the action is really taking place. The promoter earns a little extra money on booth fees, which is his only real interest.

The customers who attend these shows come with a specific mindset: They are geared to look at cars or furniture or attend the rodeo. Craft quality is usually poor and the crowds in attendance are not there to shop. A full day of entertainment with the kids is on the agenda. All kinds of expensive food is available, there are carnival rides for the children and young adults, and the beer and wine are flowing. Customers have planned their day and their budget to include admission and parking fees, and they plan to spend a bundle of money on food, drink, rides, and the main attraction. They have no money left to buy your product.

Unless your product is food, the food and gift promotion will probably also be a flop for you. This promotion is a showcase for commercial enterprises, specialty shops, and gimmick appliances. You may find yourself sandwiched in between a vendor selling a new carving knife and another demonstrating a blending machine. The promoter has spent a lot of money renting a big convention center and she wants to fill every available inch of space. If you have a craft you can demonstrate, and therefore compete with a tomato slicer on one side and a stereo system on the other, you may survive, but rarely.

Rod and gun shows and antique car shows present the same problems. They are very specific to the customers they are seeking to attract. Of course, they want anyone who will pay an admission fee at the door and so will include crafts as an extra added attraction. Some wives who have no interest in guns, fishing rods, or antique cars will come along with their husbands, and the craft show will keep them occupied, but how much they spend is another matter, as hubby is spending all their money elsewhere at the show. So we suggest you avoid this kind of promotion.

Prime rib and chili cook-offs may be just a Western thing, but similar events involving other kinds of food take place in other parts of the country. We will not speculate on what success you may find elsewhere, but in California and Nevada these shows can be devastatingly poor for craft artists—particularly in Nevada.

Usually a gambling casino hires a promoter to put on a show in the parking lot or out in front of the casino. The promoter has established a long tradition. The show is just another gimmick to draw people into the casino where they'll blow their money. But, those same people won't spend much of that money in your craft booth. The ribs and chili are supposedly in competition, and these food booths attract the hungry who may be competing for some sort of prize. Seemingly potential customers are, in reality, only passersby stopping to fill their face on their way into the casino. We did one such show, made $235 in three days, lost our shirt (even without going into the casino, since we had no money to gamble), and never did a show like that again. Finally, you have the local club functions and charity events. These can be either highly successful or a real disappointment, but are well worth researching. The application fee is usually relatively low—$50 to $75. Oftentimes they have a long-standing, traditional following. Most are just advertised locally, but if they are run by a big church, for example, they are generally well promoted and have a solid tradition behind them. These kinds of shows will usually draw large crowds who are there to buy. Church events can be particularly profitable because the priest, minister, or rabbi has been promoting the show from the pulpit for weeks, and the congregation feels obligated to attend and spend money to support the function.

These can be especially pleasant shows to do because the clientele are always well behaved. The people attending aren't going to get drunk. The promoters are members of the club or church who are volunteering their time and who usually run just this one show a year. The atmosphere is always cordial, friendly, and homespun. They'll provide coffee and doughnuts in the morning, help you set up your booth, offer to fill in for you if you need a break, and serve you lunch if you're there alone. These shows always have a genuine family atmosphere in which socializing with the customer is a pleasure. You should always choose carefully among these promotions, as their warmth and friendliness can't compensate for a lost financial weekend. But when they are great, as was the last show we ever did, these promotions are a genuine joy.

The same can be said for craft shows being put on by service organizations like the Lions Club or the Elks. As we mentioned earlier, most of the time you will find these organizations involved in large, community-promoted shows, but sometimes they will run their own show, particularly in smaller towns. The potential negatives of that kind of show have already been discussed but, once in a while, if you want to or have a need to take a gamble, you will find a "sleeper" that will provide you with sufficient profit to make the trip worthwhile. They are always well supported by the membership and always very happy, pleasant shows in which to take part.

Obviously, a craftsperson's "heaven," the perfect show, would include guaranteed, ideal weather conditions and a space location where you could drive your truck right up to your booth space to unload and load. Your truck would always be loaded with an excess of inventory, all of which you sell to a large crowd, all of whom were spending their money extravagantly. You would head home with a big two-day profit after saying thank-you to the promoters who, given all these heavenly conditions, must have done everything right, including stopping by to introduce themselves, thanking you for participating, and asking if you are happy and content with everything. Occasionally, we found all this but, for the most part, we have to live and die to go to heaven.

7

Booth Setup
and Booth Display

THROUGHOUT THIS BOOK, MOST OF THE EMPHASIS HAS
been placed on subjects involved primarily with your craft—the effort
and money management involved in producing it, and the means by
which you may present it to the world and sell it. Judy and I have tried to share
as many of the tricks of the trade regarding these subjects as we can think of, and
if you are a beginner and you have sent out those applications and been notified
of your acceptance into various shows, you are almost in the crafts business.

If you are a veteran and have gone through the application and exhibition
procedure many times, the word *beginner* still applies to you to some extent if
your booth, like so many hundreds we have seen, has not had the benefit of all
of your talent, attention, and creativity. Until you sell your craft, you are still
creating for art's sake, still engaging in a hobby—albeit one with a new purpose. Likewise, you can be a veteran in the crafts business, but if you have given
absolutely no attention to your booth display, you've been shortchanging yourself and your potential customers.

The Neglected Craft Booth

If, as a longtime craftsperson, all you have done—or think you need to
do—is erect a canopy over your head, set up a few tables or pedestals, set out a
meager selection of your wares, and hope for the best (and complain about the
worst), you are as much a novice as the person who has never sold at all. Booth
display, as every good promoter agrees, separates those who are accepted from
those who are rejected from their shows. If you have neglected this part of your
business or do not apply yourself to it, you have missed or will miss a major

opportunity that is open to you. You will remain a novice, or an amateur, until that first day when you put yourself and your craft, professionally displayed, out there on the line to truly compete with everyone else in the business.

If you are ready to so compete, you are also now ready to deal with what we consider the most crucial factor of your business, second only to your product. That factor is the booth from which you are going to sell your merchandise and the method you are going to use to display it.

We don't know why, but we can say with absolute certainty that the following is true: With the exception of those competing at the highest level of the industry, craftspeople sorely neglect the tasks of creating beautiful and yet highly functional booths and setting up inviting displays of crafts in those booths. For some reason, all too often, some of the most beautiful, imaginative, and creative crafts are so poorly displayed that the artistry of their creator is completely lost.

Judy and I have viewed thousands upon thousands of craft booths over the years, and the biggest percentage of them demonstrate a total lack of creativity, imagination, or sensitivity. We have speculated that perhaps it is because some craftspeople develop tunnel vision through which they see only the beauty of their craft—the individual piece of work—but not the totality and surroundings in which they exhibit it. Perhaps it reflects a kind of mental or artistic fatigue, developed after so much energy has gone into creating the craft itself. Or, maybe it comes down to just a "take it or leave it" attitude. Whatever it is, the failure to devote creative energy to the presentation of the product is largely responsible for a craftsperson's failure to sell as much as he should. We strongly urge you to spend a great deal of time considering what is explained in this chapter, studying the photographs on the following pages, and then to apply what you read and see to the creation or re-creation of your craft booth.

Your Booth Is Your Store

Every craftsperson should realize that you don't just sell your product. There is a great deal more to consider and accomplish before those exciting days when you actually sell your merchandise. There are many obstacles to face and hurdles to overcome before you set up your booth. Some are practical, others are physical, and many more are aesthetic.

As you begin the process of booth planning and construction, we would suggest that you think of it as creating your own little world, a ten-by-ten-foot shop, an environment into which you are inviting the public and also one in which you will be comfortable, and of which you will be proud. We can assure you that the time, effort, and money you put into this project will yield big dividends. For an example of how important Harvest Festival considers booth display, take a look at the promoter's regulations found on the following pages.

Booth Set-up

Here's What We Do For You:

- We provide a curtained 8' back wall, 500 watts of electricity, and 24-hour security.

- Back walls of booths have neutral-toned curtains.

- Standard booth spaces are 10' wide, but *flexibility* is the key! You could end up with part of a pillar or pole in your booth. Some decorator supports have large bases, which you may have to work around. You should design your booths to be 9'6" wide to allow for extra flexibility. Depths vary from 8' to 10'. Refer to the floor plan for information specific to each city.

Here's What We Need From You:

- We require that you provide a minimum of 7' side and back walls—**a maximum of 8'**. Side walls help you and your neighbors present your crafts in your own unique storefront; and make the whole show more attractive to customers. Your front facade can be a maximum of 12' high. Only 50% of the roof can be covered.

- When fully constructed, your booth must be flexible to allow for a 4–6" deviation from the width of the assigned space to allow for pillars and unforeseen floor plan irregularities. Always measure your booth from front to back and side to side **before** you set up.

- Side walls must be opaque hard walls or flameproofed fabric. If you use lattice or grids you must use fabric to cover the backs of the walls.

- Provide carpet or floor covering. We suggest linoleum for food exhibitors.

- We encourage the use of company name signs in your booth. However, **vinyl signs are prohibited**, and the signs must not exceed the 8' side and back wall heights.

- Cash registers may be used, but in keeping with the "handmade" nature of our shows, they should be concealed from the customer's view. Consider building a special area into your booth to house a cash register and your bags. We recommend this for security reasons as well.

- Spreading your product and display into the aisle is prohibited. You must stay completely within the 8x10'or 10x10' space assigned.

DISPLAY YOUR BOOTH NUMBER. The show directories for customers are useless without visible booth numbers, and you can lose important sales!

- Special sales and discounts will, in most cases, be discouraged as they tend to detract from the overall quality. If you reduce the price of an item during the show replace the price tag instead of crossing out the old price.

- **No K-D canopy or E-Z up type tops.** If you are using the frame of your outdoor set-up, convert it into an indoor set-up. Cover all exposed metal with fabric sleeves or garlands, remove the plastic side and back walls and replace them with attractive flameproofed material.

- No hand-drawn signs are allowed unless it is done by calligraphy.

- Use a tarp or bed sheet to cover the front of your booth at night when you leave.

- Fire Marshals require that all extension cords be heavy duty: 3-pronged/grounded type.

- A 6-outlet power strip is required, which plugs into the electrical outlet provided behind your booth. Turn off the lights by the main power strip's on/off switch.

The above regulations are MANDATORY. Show management reserves the right to enforce them as needed at the exhibitor's expense.

Electrical Notes

500 watts of electricity is **included** in your booth fee. If you require additional electricity, please contact the electrician for your city on the All-City Reference Chart.

- A back drape is provided for you. If you require side walls, uprights, bases, carpet or other equipment, contact the decorators listed on the All-City Reference Chart.

- **For advance payment discount price to apply, payment must be received by the outside contractors with your order by the deadline date.**

Creating a Fantastic Booth

We can recite success story after success story to you about artists who re-designed their booths to enhance their crafts. Here are some tips that are easy and effective:

• Use signage! Attractive, colorful signs and banners help people remember who you are and where you're located. Remember, the quality of your signage reflects on the quality of your craft.

• Props—antiques, accent pieces and photos of the craft-making process, for instance— add a nice finishing touch and add flair!

*Remember that free booth evaluations are available one-on-one with Yvonne Chilina at the shows. Sign up sheet is in the Show Office.

Loading & Unloading

Normal set-up is 9AM–8PM Thurs. (Other than exception listed on All-City Reference Chart, no early set-ups are permitted). Load-in closes promptly at 8:00PM. If you break down on the way, please call our office (707-778-6300), get the phone number for our show office, and leave a message there so we can arrange for your late arrival. *If you do not call by 6PM of set-up day, your booth space is subject to cancellation without a refund, please see contract.*

■ As soon as you arrive at the hall, go to the Harvest Festival check-in area located in each hall beginning at 9AM on set-up day. You'll find all the essentials here: updated show information including your booth assignment (be sure to double check this), exhibitor badges, unloading/parking/storage instructions and a warm welcome!

■ Bring a dolly or hand cart! The halls do not provide these for exhibitor use. You will not be able to bring your vehicle into the hall to unload.

■ Loading/unloading procedures differ in each city due to hall access irregularities. To save yourself any frustration, please check with staff before you begin. If you are on the loading dock, please follow this procedure during load-in as a courtesy to your fellow craftspeople:
1. Unload booth and merchandise quickly.

2. Remove your vehicle **immediately** to allow others to have hall access. **Vehicles left unattended are subject to being towed at owner's expense.**
3. Return to construct booth and arrange stock.

■ As you set up, please be courteous to your neighbors— keep aisles clear.

■ **Teardown begins after 6PM closing time Sunday.** (Check the All-City Reference Chart for show hours.) *There are no early tear downs!* Please be considerate of our paying customers and fellow artists by observing this rule.

■ For load-out, simply reverse the procedure!
1. Box your stock.
2. Tear down your booth.
3. Check with Festival show team to see if a loading pass is required.
4. Retrieve your vehicle, load your booth & stock quickly.

■ Load-out must be completed by midnight Sunday night (Monday for Long Beach).

Note: San Diego, San Francisco and San Jose halls all have particularly difficult load-ins. Please be prepared and maintain your patience! You can help others by unloading your vehicle and removing your car or van from the unloading area quickly.

One of the many practical problems you face is investing in both an indoor and outdoor setup. This is more complicated than you may imagine. Have you gone to many crafts shows or taken part in many and seen hundreds of booths set up? Have you ever considered the hours and money that are invested in developing a professional-looking booth? Maybe you have and for just that reason have decided not to create one. If so, you've made a serious financial miscalculation. You were being penny wise and dollar foolish.

The types of canopies that will protect you and your merchandise from sun and wind and rain outdoors are quite simple. At outdoor shows, you have probably seen many variations of such protective enclosures. In reality, these structures are as important to the display of your work as the frame is to a painting.

Many such booths are simply four upright and four horizontal plastic or metal pipes, sometimes supporting a tarpaulin stretched across the top for protection against the rain and sun. In other cases, as in the photograph below, the Seydel booth is supporting a vast array of wind chimes and no tarpaulin is used. Though not in this example, the upright poles are usually set in a can of cement as a way to weight them down against the wind.

These homemade setups, for which you need only purchase piping and corner connectors, are often used by craftspeople who are either not involved in the business at the most professional, weekly level, or, as in the case of the Seydels, it is simply the most expeditious way to present their beautiful wind

chimes, a craft that defies almost every other means of being displayed. It serves their needs as no other booth can do, but is pretty much out of favor with most craftspeople, since it presents some problems that the Seydels choose to risk.

While a little wind may be advantageous to the sale of chimes, too much wind will destroy the effect. The booth also offers them no protection from sun and rain, and as it is so filled with merchandise that these merchants must find seating somewhere outside the booth. Though the photograph does not make it evident, there are aisles within the booth through which the customer may ramble for better viewing and selection of each chime.

You will also see at outdoor shows a more modern version of a covered booth—a sun canopy that can be purchased in major outlets like K-Mart, Wal-Mart, Home Base, and other such stores. These are semi-pyramid-shaped, with a nylon or acrylic canopy that is stretched across the top and down to the base of each pole. They come in many colors, are easily set up, and homeowners are beginning to use them on their patios and lawns. No example of this could be found at the time we were shooting photographs. Hopefully, you are familiar with what is being described.

On the plus side, these canopies are lightweight and less expensive than the next type we will describe, but they have a number of drawbacks: While they will screen out some sun a good part of a very hot day, they are very unstable, even in a moderate wind, and offer no real protection from the wind and cold and rain. Though they are simple enough to assemble, their assembly actually takes more time than the assembly of any other type of outdoor booth.

Most common nowadays is the fold-up, accordion-fashion, metal booth that tapers to a peak at the top. It spreads out to a ten-by-ten-foot booth and is adjustable in height up to twelve feet, yet the booth collapses into a rectangle, approximately four feet long and a foot square, with the canvas top still attached, making it very portable and compact. You can purchase a canvas carrying case along with four nylon or canvas detachable and zip-up sides that can all be packed into a separate bag. This has to be purchased at special outlets or can be found advertised in many craft magazines. This outdoor booth is quite a bit more expensive than the booths mentioned above (in the $500 range), but is unquestionably your best option.

For our first few years we used the other types, wasted money, suffered the indignities they cause, and finally realized that they did not enhance our product and so were reducing our selling potential. We decided that the expense of this new booth was a worthwhile investment. They are extremely durable: Ours lasted thirteen years and we only had to purchase one new canopy top during those years.

At any outdoor show, you are subject to the elements on any given day. It is to your physical and mental benefit to be properly and completely prepared, so that you and your product are as invulnerable as possible. The four upright posts can be staked into the ground or weighted or both. All four canvas sides can either be rolled up or zipped closed and the front canvas even has a zipper doorway. Erecting this booth should take no more than fifteen minutes and will be the easiest part of the entire set-up process. You will notice in the photographs that almost every booth that is cited as a good example uses this type of canopy.

Catastrophes, Inconveniences, and Means of Preventing Them

We are spending a lot of time on this aspect of your booth setup, not just to give you the best advice that can be given on types of booths available and in use, but also because we wish to contribute to your own ease and comfort and peace of mind.

Your booth will be your home for ten to twelve hours a day, two or three days each week. On two occasions, we had our earliest booths ripped apart by vicious winds; one was actually blown up in the air and dropped on another craftsperson's booth. More than once I stood in the center of the booth, surrounded by customers seeking shelter from the driving wind and rain, holding the booth down, while Judy tried to sell our baskets.

These are very agonizing experiences, as you can imagine. Those scenarios make for very long, nerve-wracking, and tension-producing days. There is not a moment that you will be able to relax, even if there isn't a customer in your booth or anywhere in sight. It is extremely rare that weather conditions are so bad that a promoter will close down a show, so you will still be there holding down your booth in the storm while most of the customers have gone home.

At another craft show, the wind and driving rain kept blowing our merchandise off the shelves because our booth had no sides. Judy and I spent the day picking up baskets, returning them to the shelves, or trudging to the truck with wet and damaged goods. On one such trip, I also slipped in the mud and severely sprained my ankle, adding to the agony of the weekend. That night we had to dry out every basket at the motel. That same weekend we watched as another person's entire display of stained glass—some $5,000 worth—was blown to smithereens.

Because these kinds of incidents are so common, we strongly recommend the type of canopy we have described. Not only is setup much faster and easier, but there is the speed of teardown in emergencies and the security that this type of booth affords. At many street fairs in which you will take part, you have to take down and set up your booth both days because the street is re-opened to automobile traffic at night. Or even if the street remains closed, it is still open to the public, which means your booth would be vulnerable to thieves and vandalism. This type of booth reduces the time that you have to spend tearing down.

In other instances, the promoter provides security personnel who walk the show site all night long. This very helpful service enables you to leave all your merchandise set up in your booth. You can just zip up the sides and go off to dinner and your motel feeling a sense of security about your property and without having to pack everything up each day.

The open-type canopy also leaves you vulnerable to an overnight rain or snowstorm. There is no worse feeling than sitting in your motel at night, a driving storm outside, knowing that the next morning you will find everything soaking wet and blown over. Much better is the sense of security that all your hard work has not been wasted, your product has not been destroyed, and everything will be intact. The sense of relief you will feel is indescribable when you arrive at the show site on Sunday morning to see other booths literally hanging in the treetops or blown up the street, while yours is sitting there as it was the day before, waiting only for you to open it up, put your money in the cash register, and begin greeting your customers.

Your Display for Outdoor Setup

Depending on your craft, there are probably endless ways that you may choose to design the interior of your booth so that it displays your craft to its best advantage. In considering that, you should simultaneously be conceiving of a way to exhibit and store as much of your inventory as is possible. Since just putting out your stock for display will consume most of your set-up time, you want to design the inside of your booth in such a way as to make this activity as simple and non-time-consuming as possible. So, long before you ever drive to the craft show, you should have worked all this out, particularly since you sent a picture of your booth to the promoter, didn't you?

Some merchandise is best displayed on shelves that you will have to either buy or build. Pottery, as displayed in this next photo (opposite page, top) created by Carol Henschieb, is an excellent example. The shelving is tiered at various levels, which allows each piece to stand alone as an example of her work, her particular artistic technique, and the colors she emphasizes. The simple bamboo backdrop allows her booth to be easily assembled and provides the appropriate color background for her work. Notice that she does not crowd the booth with so much merchandise that nothing is really seen. While this may seem to contradict what was said earlier about providing the customer with a vast selection from which to choose, in this case that advice does not apply because she is emphasizing the uniqueness of each of her pottery items as an artistic piece. Yet she still displays a wide variety of individual pieces and you can be sure that, stored on the shelf covered with bamboo, she has many more pieces.

The photograph on the opposite page, bottom, is another excellent example of how shelving can be arranged beautifully and functionally in a small

space. Every type of stained glass lampshade and lamp is visible at just a glance into the booth. Take note of the small, stained glass items—primarily night lights—set in the racks on the righthand side of the booth. These are the less expensive items that Debbie Pirole can depend on selling at shows where the much more expensive merchandise is moving slowly. Notice, too, the simplicity of the shelves on which the merchandise is placed and how much room is left for the customer to roam and browse; yet thousands of dollars worth of Debbie's craft is on display. Though you cannot see it in this photograph, at the rear left is a counter and chair from which she conducts business.

Clothing requires racks and hangers on which to hang the clothing and usually a booth within a booth, where people can try on your dresses or jackets or T-shirts. Nancy Lee Kaufman's booth, photograph below, is a very tasteful and professional clothing booth. Since the clothing she produces does not require privacy in order to try it on, there is no dressing room, and she utilizes the space at the rear left as her business area. There is a mirror in which the customers may view themselves—something that is necessary for selling this kind of craft. Nancy's booth has a nicely balanced effect: It is not congested with clothing, and there is plenty of room for a number of people to survey what is on each rack, while simultaneously presenting all the designs and fashions in which she specializes.

Artwork, prints, and wall decorations require walls on which they can be displayed. If you are a jeweler, jewelry of fine quality necessitates glass cases and stands on which to put them. A particularly good example of such a booth is that of Maraya, found in the photograph on the opposite page. The propri-

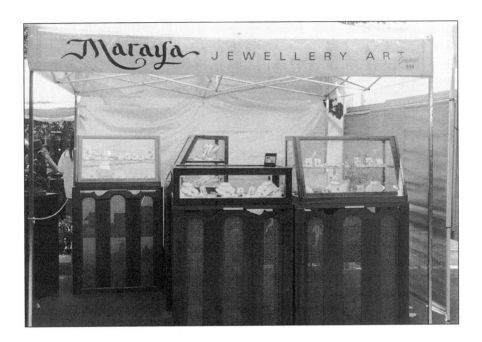

etor's name is prominent, and the credit cards she accepts are displayed in front. The workmanship of the stands and cases alone catches the eye and draws you into her booth. Unfortunately, as I mentioned, photographing jewelry is a real skill, so you will have to take my word that Maraya's is exquisite. We particularly like this booth setup because it combines the ability to view her work from the outside, while inviting the customer into the booth to look further, unlike many jewelry merchants who display only at the front.

Sculpture is usually displayed on pedestals—or should be. To place fine sculpture on crowded, poorly lit shelves would be to lose the essence of the particular work. Jeff Tritel's absolutely superb pieces, the top photograph on the following page, are the best example we could find.

Nothing fancy here—that is the nature of Jeff's art. Each piece stands out starkly against a plain white backdrop, and each piece can be viewed from every angle. Whether everyone likes Jeff's sculpture is, of course, a matter of personal taste, but only the most insensitive could fail to appreciate his talent.

The second photograph on the following page represents the work of a woman who is new to the crafts business. Judy and I spent a good deal of time conversing with this husband and wife team. Her work represents replicas of Native American art and is extremely well-done. She appeals to a limited market and is going to have find her niche in the craft world. This booth is representative of someone starting out in the business: She has the beginning of an idea as to how best present her work, but she is not quite there yet. She told us

that she was having trouble at this stage producing enough inventory; some pieces were selling very fast and others weren't selling at all. She has a large variety but, because no two were alike, her problem was compounded. She might be better off focusing on producing those pieces that have already proven themselves as desirable, or the business may become too wearing. She has a very unusual product. We wish her well.

The booth of Nancy and Julien Williams, photograph above, is an excellent example of how to handle a special problem encountered by craftspeople who sell handmade dolls, rabbits, bears, and whatever else may be stuffed. All in one booth, Nancy and Julien use tables, hangers, shelves, and furniture (also for sale) on which the rabbits sit. Small items hang from the slatted partitioning and even from the canopy itself. In the back is a counter; behind that is a chair. Yet the booth is clean, neat, and offers the customer plenty of room in which to shop. All in a ten-by-ten-foot space. Underneath and behind them there is also storage space. A booth could not be more compactly designed and has another feature to be discussed with the booth in the top photograph on the following page.

I doubt that we can provide a better example of the ultimate booth than that owned by Jim and Louise Howes, whose business name is Rabbit Run. This is the small shop referred to earlier. The consummate charm and warmth of this booth is self-evident. Everything in it and on the walls is for sale, yet everything looks as if it were part of a permanent establishment. Creating this effect takes talent, time, and money, but be assured that it contributes immensely to their sales. There isn't a promoter in existence who wouldn't want this booth in his show. That fact is evident in the second photograph on the following page. Here the booth is displayed at a Country Folk Art indoor show. With the canopy removed and the addition of interior lighting, which cannot be seen in the photograph, the top and sides provide further means of displaying an even greater variety of their wood products while enhancing the appearance and

overall effectiveness of their booth. Booth (see photograph, previous page) can also be converted to indoor shows with the same simplicity.

In a category all its own, the photograph on the next page is a good example of a method of selling a craft that is utterly unique. Granted, the craftsper-

son cannot display a great deal of her merchandise, and usually this type of movable cart is most appropriate at indoor shows and malls. However, it still works fine at quaint, picturesque street fairs, as depicted in the top photograph on the following page, a summer street fair in Nevada City, California.

Finally, the bottom photograph on the following page, "Gatherings," by Rhoda Paul, is very illustrative of a typical outdoor display of floral arrangements. Various pieces are hung, others are distributed about the floor space, readily accessible and easy to observe. The trelliswork—often used with floral displays—is both functional and serves aesthetically to reduce the bland effect of the needed, but boring canopy.

These photographs should give you a good idea of what is recommended for outdoor setups, and you no doubt have seen many such booths in person. Your goal, then, is to devise the best way to display your product, all within a ten-by-ten-foot space—the largest that most craftspeople lease. You will see larger booths, because some craft artists need more room to display all their inventory. Some will pay for two, side-by-side, ten-foot spaces—at double the booth fee, of course.

Double booth space requires that you double your inventory to fully stock two booths and double your shelving or whatever you use to display your craft. Naturally, this usually necessitates a larger vehicle to transport all that equipment and inventory. And it goes without saying that it is necessary to sell that much more of your product to defray the additional cost.

Your Indoor Booth Display

The top photograph picturing Weathervane Capital's booth, and the bottom photograph, the booth created by Gable's Country Basket, are good examples of the use of double space at an indoor craft show. Weathervane Capital

takes an interesting and novel approach by creating an outdoor yard display, complete with picket fence. The business counter does not detract from the effectiveness of the craft presentation and, most unusual, in this rare case, there is no need to enter the booth at all. Every weather vane is right out there to be seen by the customer and is within easy reach. Gable's, while providing a great deal of interior walking room, also presents crafts in total view of the public with easy access. In both cases, the business name selected is also memorable.

Some long-established craftspeople eventually find it necessary and very profitable to expand in this way, but we never were capable of attaining that manufacturing level. We recommend that you should be well into the business before you attempt this larger marketing approach.

Remember, too, that while we said a ten-by-ten-foot space is the standard size booth, that size space can only be relied on at outdoor shows, which accommodate the standard-size canopy. Because your space at some indoor shows may be smaller, you must be able to reduce or expand your booth size as each situation presents itself. Flexibility—on your part and in the design of your booth—is the key. When you have developed and set up your booth, you must remember to allow room for a counter on which to carry out your monetary transactions and at least one chair. Standing on your feet is not an option, particularly after a long drive starting at four in the morning and setup immediately upon arrival.

Yet, having advised that, you will notice in the photographs that many do not have such a counter. Some artisans would rather sacrifice their personal comfort for the extra room to display their product, or will simply walk in and out of the booth all day, standing to the side when it is crowded, and transact their financial dealings from either a small register placed somewhere in the booth or from a money belt. We don't recommend the latter, but, in the final analysis, it comes down to whatever works for you.

The same applies to what has been said about crafts, like jewelry, that are often displayed only at the front of the booth, primarily to catch the customer's eye. Food booths, selling candy, soups, jellies, and jams, may offer samples for the customer to taste and buy; craftspeople who are continually demonstrating their product may also follow this setup design. So many choose to display in this manner, rather than opening up the interior of their booth space, because food can be sampled from the aisle as people pass by. So, while it does congest the aisles, everyone has to do what's necessary to make a living. These types of vendors will always have an easier and faster setup than you will. However, for most in the business, that easy a setup is not a viable or even recommended alternative. We suggest that you study the photographs on the pages of this chapter closely. You will have to judge them for yourself and decide which setup styles work for you. As you note the effort and expense that goes into designing and setting up many of these booths, you will realize that creating a new booth or revamping your old one is not a simple task.

If you think you have created a wonderful outdoor booth that is versatile enough to work anywhere—including the great indoors—you will have to reconsider that idea. Most of the time, you will find that your outdoor canopy is not at all suitable for the indoor shows you will do. Very few good indoor shows even allow you to set up your outdoor canopy inside. Your shelving and counter or tables are convertible to your indoor booth, but not the canopy.

If you carefully examine the photographs of indoor booths, you will see that most are enclosed in such a way as to separate them from their neighbors on either side and behind. Old Ranch House Creations, photograph below, uses the very cabinets being sold as such a divider. Additional cabinets stand against the side of the booth and are stored behind it. The cabinets are made of recycled wood and hardware, and no two are identical. We bought one after taking the picture.

Unlike an outdoor show, an indoor show attempts to create the impression that you are walking up and down a street, looking into individual shops. In fact, Harvest Festival hangs flags at the end of every aisle with street names on them. Many artisans erect wooden paneling with shelving built out from the walls, from which crafts may also be hung. Others, like Mercantile Store, a

booth by Haseford Gifts and Creations, seen in photograph (left), use lattice siding, which complements the fine wood decorations the artisans produce. Notice the business counter at the left front and how well it blends in with everything else in the booth—so much so that it might be for sale.

Cottage Crafts, the top photo on the opposite page, another double booth that uses a horizontal lattice to separate the booth from its neighbors, exemplifies one of the most beautiful and elegant uses of space we have seen. Ron and Debbie Uhlack, only three years in the business, have achieved what some craftspeople never approach in their entire career. Not only is their craftsmanship superior, but the booth has a freshness and sense of openness that just invites people in. Their overhead frame allows for lighting to be attached.

If you cannot build a booth of the above type, or your craft does not lend itself to that style, at the very least you will need to devise a way to hang fire-retardant drapery around your booth, drapery that adds color or background or depth, and so enhances your craft. The name of the booth in the bottom photograph on the opposite page is Display Excellence by Kris Gibson, and a more appropriate name couldn't have been found. Using simple, white drapery as a background, Kris designed an unusual, staggered-shelving effect that allows the lighting at the top center of the booth to completely illuminate every piece

on display. Since his booth was situated on a corner, he also was able to eliminate drapery on the left side of his booth, allowing customers to view his merchandise from almost every vantage point. Following are instructions for flameproofing.

Flameproofing Requirements

All booth material must be flame retardant: decorations, drapes, banners, acoustical materials, plastic cloth, etc. Bamboo or straw is not allowed in any hall. Merchandise and any wood thicker than $^1/_{16}$" does not need to be flameproofed. All table coverings, fabric walls, paper, or any decorative material must have a flameproof certificate or tag, and you must attach the tag to the material in a prominent spot in easy view of the Fire Marshal. Flame retardant treatments must be renewed as necessary, and after each cleaning. It is your responsibility to submit proof of this to the Fire Marshal.

Note: The importance of adherence to Fire Marshal codes is obvious. To do otherwise endangers everyone. **If you fail to meet Fire Marshal regulations, we will not be able to allow you to operate your booth, and no refund will be given.** All cities require a Flame Proof Certificate. We strongly urge you to obtain one. If you don't have a certificate, be prepared for a patch test. Refer to the All-City Reference Chart on the inside back cover for the phone number of each city's Fire Marshal.

> To test for flame retardancy, hold a wooden match to a 2" X 4" fabric swatch (the thickest part, such as a hem) for 12 seconds. The flame should go out when the match is removed. If it does not, you will need to re-treat or have it commercially treated.

Permits

The following activities require permits; you must be sure to obtain them from the local fire marshal not less than 30 days in advance of the show:

- Display or operation of any heater, barbecue, heat-producing device, open flame, **candles**, lamp lanterns, torches, etc.

- Display or operation of any electrical, mechanical or chemical device which may be deemed hazardous by the Fire Department.

- Use or storage of flammable liquids, compressed gasses or dangerous chemicals.

It is the exhibitor's responsibility to obtain any special permits required for craft demonstration.

Fabric Flameproofing

We strongly recommend you purchase pre-treated, inherently flameproof fabric. This will save you the time, expense and worry of re-treating and certifying your fabrics after each cleaning. Good sources are:

Flourish Company   Dealers Supply Inc.
501-677-3300   800-524-0576

If you do purchase conventional fabric, keep in mind that the more absorbent a material, the easier it is to treat. Natural fibers are your best bet.

To have your fabrics professionally treated, check the Yellow Pages under "Flame Proofing" or call your local Fire Dept.

You may also treat fabrics yourself after each cleaning, providing you are sure to saturate well and that you test the thickest part of the material carefully after treatment.

Fire retardant spray is available for purchase at the show office.

Commercial fire-retardant is available from:

California Flameproofing and Processing, Inc.
170 North Halstead Street
Pasadena, CA 91107
626-792-6981

Dealers Supply Inc.
800-524-0576

Elaine Martin Company
P.O. Box 674
Deerfield, IL 60015-0674
800-642-1043

The effort to create a warm, charming, quaint atmosphere, photograph below, was its own reward for Carol Wickham and Jo Ann Reynolds. Their booth, called My Sister and I, combines their talents. They have created a small-shop atmosphere in which the customer feels automatically at home and at ease. This booth contributes to the overall feeling the promoter desires to create.

Some convention centers provide individual enclosures with drapery, but most do not. If you bring your own, you must set up with some sort of portable piping that you can erect and on which you can hang your own drapery or paneling. Lightweight, snap-together sets of such aluminum piping can be purchased out of most craft magazines. The pipes come in different lengths so you can vary the height and width.

If you've ever attended a top-of-the-line indoor craft show, you will remember seeing beautifully structured booths with ornate, carved, wooden facades, interior paneling, exquisite drapery, and the like. Every booth in such shows is not as grand as those, but you can bet that those are the ones that attracted the most customers. Such booths require a great deal of advanced planning, skill to construct, space to transport, and more time to erect, but they pay big dividends. Most craftspeople have to find a happy medium between the extremely elegant booth and the serviceable.

At the early stage of your craft career, you may not be ready to become involved in all this. But it is the direction in which you should set your sights if you want to be really successful. Of course, you don't necessarily have to create something quite as artful as we have described. We didn't. The promoter is looking for booths that will enhance the overall attractiveness of the show. The garden variety, flea market setup will not get you into Harvest Festival or any other show of that caliber. Aim for something substantial, functional, and still attractive. You can build the interior of your booth out of wood, metal, plastic, or whatever you may invent that separates and distinguishes you from your neighbors. Here is another place to put your creative ability to work.

Pumpkin Patch, by Dian Hall, photograph below, is a very good example of a creative approach to booth design. Simple piping has been used and then covered with valances that slide on. A light bar in the center illuminates the booth, which also draws light from the hanging lights of the hall in which the show is taking place. Metal grids strapped together are erected and used to hang the artisan's work. She has used her product hanging on the grids as the divider between her booth and her next-door neighbor's. Throw rugs in the booth set it off nicely, though I would have some concern about people tripping on them. Notice how well Dian has distributed all the various pieces she creates—some hung, some stacked, some sitting in baskets. Her small "boutique" in which the customer can roam and browse, is created without great expense.

Booth Design Is a Daunting Task

If you have a lot of talent as a designer and constructor of such things, perhaps you will find building an appropriate booth quite simple. I did not.

During our first five years in the business, I know I built at least five different booths, a new one each year. Finally, I came up with one that really worked for us. Creating an interior setup that could be used both outdoors and indoors, and is adjustable to various configurations of space is not a simple task. Just taking into account the changing dimensions required by promoters was asking for more talent than I initially possessed. At times, I was sure I needed a degree in architecture and another in engineering. If you are no more skilled than I, you may have to do it by trial and error, as I did.

One way to help create your desired, finished booth is to establish a theme. Virtually all the booths pictured thus far do this to varying degrees, and that is why they are successful. We explained how ours came about at the beginning of the book. Since some big shows also require you to wear a costume, this may help you in developing your theme. A promoter has the right to refuse to allow you to set up—and may even require you to tear down—if you do not comply with the contract you signed. Once established, a theme can guide how you build the booth, what materials you use to construct it, your choice of color schemes, and whatever decorative effects you select.

Repeat customers look for your booth because it left an impression in their mind. So once you have a booth that suits all your needs, don't change it drastically unless there is some real need to do so. Even then, try to stay within the theme you have established.

That said, it must be acknowledged that for some artists and craftspeople, establishing a theme is particularly difficult, if not impossible. Artists dealing in oils or watercolors, and attempting to display a sufficient number of their paintings, cannot simply set up some walls and hang a few paintings as if their booth were a miniature art gallery. Too many paintings on a wall destroys the effect of each one, while too few amounts to wasted space. The theme has to emerge from the style, school, and medium of the paintings themselves.

Janette Jones, photograph on the following page, solves this problem very nicely by using portable, fold-up screens. These can be opened or closed to any desired degree, then placed in the booth so customers can walk through, as if they were in a gallery, viewing the paintings hung on the screens. Each screen has its own lighting, so Janette is not dependent on the lighting of the building in which she is displaying. Notice that she also offers, on a separate stand, miniatures of her work for people who cannot afford the originals.

Janette does very fine work. However, here is a good example of a problem with the jury process that requires craftspeople to submit their application with photographs. Using an expensive camera that does everything

automatically, my wife Judy still could not capture the depth and feeling of Janette's art in this photograph. Some of it seems washed out, which it is not. Until they establish their reputation with promoters, most artists like Janette are much better off jurying in person.

Clothing booths often present a similar problem. Any theme has to be established through the style and design of the clothing itself. Workmanship has to be seen and touched. It simply cannot be adequately photographed. Kathy's Klothes, seen in top photograph, opposite page, is a good example.

Kathy once used a very complicated, double booth that required customers to enter the booth to appraise her work. She has since designed a very simple, easy-to-erect booth that allows her to display her products through the use of open space, with strategically placed lighting. Most important, she can set it up alone! The type of hangers she uses enable her to present more merchandise, more easily viewed, rather than crowding everything on traditional closetlike racks. Smaller accessories, such as detachable collars and cuffs, are placed in wire trays that can be transported without having to remove every item from every tray. Drapery on two sides serves as a backdrop for many of her unique styles. Overall, there is a sense of openness and easy accessibility. When using draperies as an enclosure for your booth, keep in mind that they are almost always required to be fire retardant. You can buy such draperies from convention center suppliers.

Finally, the photograph below, is an excellent example of how to best display floral arrangements. This booth, known as California Victorian, uses grid paneling extensively, along with tables on which vases with floral arrangements are displayed. This is either a double booth or a booth and a half, but can easily be rearranged to conform to any size space available.

We particularly liked this booth because the proprietors have not attempted to cram their booth so full of floral arrangements that the customer cannot see one from another. Each piece has its place of prominence and can be seen for what it is. We wish the rich colors and fresh appeal of these freeze-dried flowers could be truly captured on film.

Loading and Packing Your Vehicle

It may seem mundane at this point, and even irrelevant to the subject of setup and display, but setting up in a smooth and relaxed fashion—as opposed to setting up in an atmosphere of confusion and tension—may be directly related to how you pack your truck and what you do or do not bring with you. The following advice may seem to be nothing more than common sense; yet, when you find yourself in a hurry to be off to a show, some of these pointers are quite easy to forget.

Always pack your vehicle so that what you need first—your collapsible canopy or whatever rigging you use to enclose your booth—can be taken out first. The same applies to every other piece of equipment you need for setup. There is nothing more aggravating than having to unload your entire vehicle, just to retrieve what you need first, and then having to tiptoe through and around everything while you are trying to set up. So remember: Your product should be the last thing you remove from your vehicle. Using the following suggestions, make yourself a checklist and use it when loading and unloading your vehicle so you forget nothing. In a rush to leave early in the morning, we would often forget a road map or money. Anxious to get on the road after the show, amid all the chaos taking place, we left many an item behind, like a shelf or a chair or a tool that we needed at the next show. Remember the rule: *First In, Last Out. Last In, First Out.* This rule applies to major items only and depends on the capacity of your vehicle; how you load your booth, merchandise, and accessories; and the arrangement of the space available to you. Like all women, my wife could always find another nook or cranny in which to put something.

All merchandise, which usually takes up the most space, should be loaded first, since it will be last out of the vehicle. Your collapsible canopy with all the paraphernalia to set it up—canvas sides, weights, shims, piping, tarps, everything for the booth—should be loaded last, so it can be taken out first. Keep your dolly or hand truck readily accessible so that you can use it to transport your booth-setup materials and your merchandise. Display tables, pedestals, shelving, racks, and chairs should be loaded so as to be next out of the truck. The cash register, charge machine, and cellular phone and counter on which to place them should come out of the truck next. They should be set up immediately, since, at outdoor shows, many customers arrive while you are still setting up. A toolbox and all tools necessary to erecting your booth need to be available for almost immediate use. A spare tire and jack should be easily accessible, if needed, without having to empty half your truck to get to it. Always carry a first aid kit and all the medication that you require, perhaps under your seat. Include sun block. Keep an ice chest with food and drink handy. This not only saves you money, but at many early morning setups, there is no place to get anything to eat or drink until the show opens. Always carry a broom, a shovel, and, sometimes, a rake, umbrellas, sun hat and sunglasses, rain gear and extra shoes, rags or towels, extra plastic tarp, and duct tape. Make yourself a small kit with such office supplies as pens, pencils, Scotch tape, extra price tags, business cards, paper clips, rubber bands, and the like.

We found that the above items were essential for outdoor shows. The following are the major items for indoor shows, in addition to most of the above. Pack your fire-retardant drapery or whatever you use as siding for you booth so that you can set it up first. Lighting equipment, power strips, and extra light bulbs, along with a 100-foot extension cord are often needed immediately. Your indoor frame from which to hang drapery or siding should be accessible first. Don't forget your carpet, cut to the size of your booth. We often forgot this, since it wasn't used for outdoor shows. Take along a small vacuum or broom to clean the booth. A small stool or a small ladder to adjust lights and hang drapery is always necessary.

This list is just a starter for you. No doubt, you will add many things to it as a result of the unique product and booth you have created and your own personal needs. And if you're wondering how you get all this into your truck or van, you have two options: Either learn to pack your vehicle better than you have in the past or buy a bigger truck. That is not meant sarcastically. Judy and I began our career carrying everything in the back of our Suburu station wagon. After buying two trucks—the second bigger than the first—we ended up with a twelve-passenger Dodge van that we gutted to fit all the items described above.

Setting Up and Show Site Conditions

Setup is very physically and emotionally demanding. More than 95 percent of the time, setup is done on the same day the show opens. Allowing at least three to five hours to set up, depending on the show site, you can then look forward to selling your product for the next nine to twelve hours, depending on the show. The first day of a show therefore, is always a very long, exhausting, and either frustrating or exhilarating day, depending on how financially successful it turns out to be.

Yes, you've arrived enthusiastically at the show, but your spirits may be quickly dampened by many of the problems you will encounter. Booth spaces may be poorly marked. Somebody may have erroneously begun setting up in your space. It may be raining or even snowing. You may arrive late at the show site and the street is jammed with vehicles being unloaded, so you are unable to drive up to your booth space. You then must wait nervously until you can unload or park your vehicle, perhaps blocks away, and transport everything by hand to your booth space.

At many convention centers, due to few spaces at the loading dock, you will be given a time to arrive and you must be on time. Even then, you may find a line of vehicles in front of you and have to wait an hour before moving up to the loading dock. You can bet that your space will be a long way from the loading dock and you may have to make twenty to thirty trips to dolly everything to your space, perhaps in and out of an elevator or climbing stairs to do so. Once you've unloaded, you must move your vehicle as soon as you can to allow another vendor to move in. This means that you will have to pile your entire setup and inventory into your ten square feet and into the aisles commingled with your neighbors, all in the same predicament. Often at convention centers, you will find large metal plates on the floor, making that area of the floor uneven. The electrical connections may be fifty or more feet away from your booth. When you set up your booth, it may bump into an overhead air duct or some other architectural obstruction.

The litany of problems spelled out above is just a small sample of the frustrations you may encounter. In essence, perfect setup conditions are the exception, not the rule. As a result, Judy and I probably had more debates, discussions, and flat-out arguments concerning the various configurations in which the shelving could be arranged than about any other subject related to the business. Every show site presents you with different challenges.

At an outdoor show, you'll find yourself at five in the morning, when it's still pitch black outside, trying to set up in the cold or even rain with a flashlight. If the show is in a park, you may not be allowed to drive your vehicle up to your booth space because the town wants to preserve the grass. Thousands of people will trample that grass into oblivion for the next two days, but you still can't drive on it. Would you guess that was one of my pet peeves? You can't find your booth space because the chalked-in numbers have been erased or because, as one idiot did, the spaces have been marked with green powdered chalk on green grass.

Eventually, you do find your space and somebody else is setting up in it. Now you hunt for the promoter to correct the error and spend half an hour finding her. Maybe you've never seen the promoter before and have no idea who you are even looking for. Nobody you talk to has a clue as to what she looks like, much less where she can be found.

You finally find the promoter, the space assignment is straightened out, and you are setting up your canopy when you discover that there's a big hump in the street, right in the middle of your space, or a sewer into which dirty water will be running all day or an oil slick you have to clean up. The wind may be whipping through your booth, but the show must go on, so you continue to work frantically until the show opens. And while you are doing this, you will often be doing it with early rising customers looking over your merchandise and engaging in friendly conversation, ready to pounce on something they want the second you have your cash register set up. In fact, we have made a lot of money this way at seven in the morning, selling directly out of the truck to anxious buyers, while setting up at the same time.

If the show is in a park, your site may be on an uneven slope or the ground may be rocky or you may be stuck in the mud or there may be a tree in your way. Since you had to preserve the damn grass to pacify those in the community who didn't want the show there in the first place, you'll be trudging through high grass, mud, or sand, or over concrete abutments. I won't mention the gross and disgusting problems you'll encounter. Just use your imagination.

There is simply no end to them. No matter how long you are in the business, there is always a new problem for which you didn't prepare. Once again, just try to be as flexible and nonchalant as possible. Since you can tell from the way I am writing this exactly how I usually reacted to these situations, do as I say and not as I did. Try to retain your sense of humor. Nobody can prepare for every possible contingency.

To this end, we have some more tips and suggestions, but we will not attempt to provide you with a checklist on how to conduct and control yourself. If you're the calm, laid-back type of individual, the kind who smiles through adversity, you don't need my help and I couldn't give it because I don't understand people like you. But, if you're like me, after numerous expletives cursing fate, go take a walk in the park. Some personality factors do deserve special attention and consideration.

Learn Your Role

If you're part of a team, after the first few shows it will become obvious which of you tends to gets agitated easily or needs only a few minor setbacks to lose his patience. We suggest that the more easily flustered one become the "gofer." He lugs everything out of the truck; assists in setting up the booth, tables, and shelves; does the heavy grunt work; helps solve all the major problems, and then disappears somewhere. Since Judy was the patient one, I made the coffee run when we reached this stage, then hunted for a friend, and stayed out of sight until Judy had everything beautifully arranged and we were ready to do business. By then, I was again ready to smile at my customers.

It took a few years of debating to eventually decide that this was the best way to conduct our business, so we suggest that you sit down and discuss it with your partner early in your craft show journey. In our case it meant that we had to agree that Judy was going to do more of the work. I agreed readily; Judy more reluctantly.

It may be that you and your partner work well together through every stage of setup. Some partners do, but most do not. Frankly, I just found myself in Judy's way as her way of arranging the booth was almost always more practical, artistic, and easier than mine. So why engage in a futile squabble that will set a negative tone for the day? Find your role and stick with it.

Indoors or outdoors, the mental strain is the same. So you have to learn how to accommodate yourself—both to the conditions in which you find yourself and to each other. Under this stress, it is too easy to make mistakes, break things, and blame everything and everybody but yourself. You are better able to evaluate your entire situation under calm conditions. Then—and only then—if you've tried to solve every possible problem and there is something that just cannot be tolerated or to which it is impossible to adjust, go to the promoter with your dilemma. Most promoters will try to help you solve your problems, if they are solvable and not of your own making.

Back to the Checklist

As I typed out the suggestions for developing your own checklist, and my mind wandered through all those upsetting catastrophes that occurred early in the morning when my patience was thin, I realized that many things on the list seem to have no apparent reason for being there. So some explanation seem in order. It constantly boggled our minds, and more often left me highly frustrated, when we discovered that we had not brought something essential to the show and, of course, found ourselves desperately in need. Usually, that meant that one of us had to stop everything to go make a purchase—or beg someone else to lend us the item. The gofer is good for that, but you still lose time. So make yourself a tool kit with all the items necessary to your special circumstances.

It seems redundant to suggest that the driver carry a map of where you are going. Every driver has a map case. And we did too. But do you know how many times we had every map except the one we needed to get where we were going? It really hurts when you are late for setup and can't get to your booth. Judy and I agreed that she was the copilot in charge of directions. I just turned right or left on her instruction. Of course, the next time we went to the same show site, I never remembered how to get there and was reminded of my forgetfulness, but I lived with it.

If your vehicle doesn't have a real spare tire (not the skimpy, modern kind that takes you all of five miles), buy one. When you get a flat tire, the gas station is always more than five miles away. I know! When you are traveling long distances and you get a flat, you may be out in the middle of nowhere. We were there. So were many other craftspeople, who have even missed the first day of a show or arrived extremely late due to a simple problem of this kind. That kind of error costs money that you can't recover.

Always carry shims for leveling. In a park or even on the street, you will never be on a flat surface. My neighbor always seemed to have the flat spot. There are countless uses for duct tape, a spare plastic tarp, rope, extension cords, light bulbs, extra weights to hold the canopy down in the wind, stakes to stake it to the ground, and the all important bungees for multiple purposes. There isn't a thing that has been mentioned that we didn't need at one time or another—and more than once, in spite of our experience. When you do as many shows as we did, some are going to fall on the wrong time of the month. Need I say more? It is very embarrassing to have to hunt around looking for another craftsperson from whom you can borrow what you need. It is like wearing a big sign saying *rookie.*

I didn't check our space assignment at one of our first indoor shows, loaded all our longest shelves in the truck and found myself borrowing a saw and cutting two feet off all my shelving when I found the booth space was eight-by-ten feet instead of the standard ten-by-ten feet. I think it was on that day—and a hundred days like it—that I asked myself how I got into the business. Judy always reminded me of my prophetic words. Of course, when we got home, I had to buy the necessary material to make an entirely new set of shelving. A very time-consuming and expensive error on my part. That is why we stress this aspect of the business.

To recap, here are some of the things that you should include on your checklist:

- Collapsible canopy
- Canvas sides for canopy
- Weights
- Tarps
- Dolly
- Display tables or shelving
- Cash register
- Charge machine
- Cellular phone
- Cash counter
- Toolbox
- Spare tire and jack
- First aid kit
- Personal medication
- Sunscreen
- Ice chest
- Broom or vacuum
- Rake for outdoor shows
- Umbrella
- Sun hat
- Sunglasses
- Rain gear
- Rags
- Duct tape
- Maps
- Rope
- Extension cords
- Light bulbs
- Bungees
- MONEY!

How to Best Display Your Product

One way or another, you will get your booth set up. However, for some reason, many craftspeople fail to design and set up their booth in a way that displays their product to its best advantage and enhances their product's beauty and salability. Some just don't seem to know how to present their work in the best light; some simply have no artistic sense; others just don't bother to pay attention to this crucial aspect of the business. Given what we all see and experience every day when we go to the shopping mall or watch television commercials, correct presentation of your product—your creation—should be the primary concern and first priority of every craftsperson. Yet, oftentimes, it isn't.

Far too many merchants with good products fail to make big money because they fall short in this area. That is why we included so many photographs of booth setup. Because of this, Judy and I now have a consulting firm, called Fresh Perspectives, specifically to conduct on-site evaluation of craft booth setup and display. Because the problems craftspeople encounter are unique to each booth and the product being displayed, we can only spell out some general guidelines.

Create a Warm, Friendly, Colorful, and Inviting Atmosphere

As you become more experienced in your observation of potential customers, you will notice that many people don't like to step over what they perceive as an imaginary line across the front of your booth. At an indoor show, it isn't even imaginary, since you should have a carpet laid across your entire booth space and this clearly defines the aisle in which the customers are walking and the entrance to your booth.

Observing this phenomenon, Judy and I eventually came to the conclusion that, for some people, stepping across that line seems to represent a statement of financial commitment. This is especially true during the early hours of the show, when the aisles are not crowded and people have more time to look, think, and consider. To a large extent, I have no doubt that it is psychological, but it exists nonetheless. It is your job to entice customers over that line.

One way is to keep your loss leader up front, just inside your booth. Just in front of the booth would be better, but you can't block the aisles with your merchandise. The loss leader will at least cause potential customers to pause, at which time you should greet them and engage them in some conversation. At that point, they will usually step across that line and you've made a beginning. After that, use your judgment to decide how much conversation to employ.

Illuminating Your Booth

At outdoor shows, lighting your booth is rarely, if ever, a problem. Find yourself facing the rising sun in the morning or the hot setting sun at night, and you'll have more light than you ever want or need. Indoor shows, on the other hand, present you with numerous lighting problems and challenges that must be overcome.

Your object is to illuminate your booth and your merchandise as well as possible, while maintaining a warm atmosphere and avoiding glaring lights that disturb the customer. Some people are particularly light sensitive and will leave the booth if a light is glaring in their eyes. Other people have trouble reading price tags, especially if the lighting is poor, and will leave the booth rather than ask the price. Refer again to the photographs to see how various booths have solved the lighting problem. For your convenience, a reference sheet, "Lighting Your Space" appears on the next page. It was provided to us by the Harvest Festival promoters and is part of their *Hands-on Show Guide*.

Most indoor facilities have overhead lighting, but these lights are rarely sufficient. Oftentimes, they err in the opposite direction: They're so glaring that they detract from the show's ambiance. This is particularly true if the craft show is in a large convention hall or an arena where the lighting is seventy-five feet or more over your head. You can see this in some of the photographs. The hall will have light, but it's not the kind of light that enhances your merchandise, brings out the color of your work, or shows your products to the best advantage.

Because the situation described above is so common, you need to invest in some kind of track lighting that you can focus from directly above your booth or attach to the sides or shelves. This will enable you to spotlight every area of the booth without shining light into your customers' eyes. Such fixtures can be purchased in any good lighting store along with the proper bulbs.

You should also purchase a few electric power strips and the 100-foot extension cord we mentioned. Most indoor facilities have outlets all over the floor, but your booth may not be close enough to one of them to plug the strip in directly. It would be a good idea if you went to a few big indoor craft shows to observe the various lighting systems used by the craftspeople with long experience. This will help you determine which system would best suit your needs. In some cases, a few small lamps, placed strategically in your booth, may also do the trick. Obviously, craftspeople who sell lamps have it made.

In order to achieve the proper effect, we set up our entire booth—complete with merchandise—at home in our living room at night. In a completely dark room, we were able to experiment with every possible variation of lighting until we found what combination worked the best for us. Harvest Festival's *Show Planning Checklist*, seen on page 145, recommends this strategy as well, along with many other good tips.

You may find, for example, that foot lighting—lights pointed from the floor upwards—or side lighting best brings out the qualities you most wish to showcase in your product. Experiment with every possible placement of the

Lighting Your Space

Overhead hall lights are dimmed or turned off at Harvest Festivals, so it is vitally important for you to create a direct lighting system within your booth to enhance your craft. Your lights should shine directly on your craft. After set-up, stand outside your booth to check your lighting from the customer's point-of-view.

Four or five spotlights should provide ample lighting for your booth. We provide 500 watts of electricity free-of-charge for each 8'x10' or 10'x10' booth; 750 watts is provided in a 15' booth and 1000 watts is provided in a 20'

booth. If you need more wattage, contact the show electrician to order it prior to your arrival (see All-City Reference Chart for name & phone).

Helpful Hint: Small halogen lights throw off 1.5 times more light than a traditional bulb, i.e. a regular 50-watt bulb puts out 50 watts of light, a 50-watt halogen bulb will throw off the equivalent of 75 watts while using only 50 watts of electricity. The halogen lights are a little more expensive but in the end you get more light for your money.

Backlighting:

Lighting from behind used in conjunction with primary accent lighting from the front. Adds depth to a three-dimensional object. Creates silhouettes. Makes volume of object more apparent and separates it from the background.

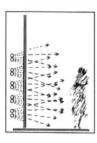

Floodlighting:

Downlighting with flood lamps to illuminate areas or walls. Appropriate when high levels of light are needed, such as to spotlight a large piece of equipment. Could also establish an upbeat, upscale mood by making the booth a flood of light on a dark show floor.

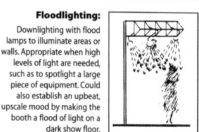

Wall Lighting:

Subtle form of floodlighting. Uses lamps mounted closely to the wall at a very shallow angle. When projected from the bottom up, makes the wall appear taller. From the bottom down, makes the wall seem firmly attached to the ground. Also accentuates textures, makes the wall appear to glow.

Spotlighting:

Accent lighting using a narrow beam lighting. The form of downlighting most used in exhibitry. Should be used sparingly to illuminate featured items 3-10 times more brightly than their surroundings. Attracts visitors & provides subdued drama.

Uplighting:

Lights are pointed upward to reflect off the ceiling, an awning or ceiling drape. Provides even light with little glare. Also known as indirect or bounce lighting. Provides cheery, bright & shadowless atmosphere, but may flatten or wash out an exhibit. Best if used with accent lighting.

Color Wash:

Using gels or filters to add color to establish contrast on a wall or floor. Presents strong visual cues to establish an atmosphere or theme.

Show Planning
CHECKLIST

Long-term planning:

☐ Make sure ALL items to be sold have been juried

☐ Order Exhibitor Discount Cards from the Harvest Festival to pass out and mail to your customers

☐ Make arrangements for shipment of your booth and inventory

☐ Obtain current seller's permits (as required) for each show city (see All-City-Reference Chart)

☐ Report your permit numbers to the Harvest Festival Customer Service Department

☐ Flame-proof all fabric and obtain a Flame Proof Certificate

☐ Plan your costume; be sure you comply with Harvest Festival dress code!

☐ Are you exhibiting in November or December? Remember to highlight your dress and decorations with Christmas accents

☐ Make your hotel (and air) or RV park reservations; note the cut-off date for Harvest Festival rooms

☐ Order pipe & drape & electrical for each show, as needed

Before You Leave Home:

☐ Test your booth set-up: set it up, check the lighting, and take a photo!

☐ Check the All-City Reference Chart for set-up, tear-down, & show hours

☐ Tune-up and winterize your vehicle.

☐ Check your booth size for each show.

Bring to the Show:

☐ Your Seller's Permits and display them at each show

☐ Your exhibitor badges to each show

☐ Your Show Guide for reference…don't leave home without it!

☐ Your Flame Proof Certificate

☐ Your most recent invoice

lights until you find the arrangement that works best to achieve your desired effect. Some photographs we have included in this chapter may help a bit, but not much, as no nonprofessional photograph—particularly in black and white—can capture the real effect of lighting. You should note, however, the various placement of lights. They may give you some ideas with which to experiment. Since no two booths are exactly alike, each craftsperson must find her own solution.

Other Lighting Problems

In some convention centers, the management turns off the overhead lights when the show starts, either to save on the electric bill or to highlight the show in a more professional manner—most often the latter. Sometimes, too, the overhead power goes out and the only light you may have is that in your booth. After all the work and effort you have put into producing your product, you want the customer to see it.

Incidentally, or maybe not so incidentally, you are paying for your electricity. Some promoters include it in the total cost of your booth space; others charge for it separately. If the charge is separate, you can choose not to hook up to an electric source thereby saving $30 or $40, but this would be a foolish way to save money. Don't forget that many shows run until nine or ten o'clock at night. You could find yourself without any lighting at all.

Without sufficient light, many people who are partially color-blind (like me) cannot distinguish colors, especially dark colors like black or navy blue or subtle shades of blue and green. Such subtleties may be the quality that most expresses the uniqueness of your product. This was the case with our baskets, as it is with all fine jewelry. Color contributes immensely to the impression made by fine pottery, where glaze and depth of pigment and paint can be so important.

So, too, with products made of glass, and especially any product involving the use of stained glass or miniaturization. At one of our last shows, there was an older woman who did the most exquisite miniature painting we had ever seen. Nobody was buying from her because, first, she should have provided a means of magnification; second, her pieces were not at eye level; and third, she did not provide any lighting. So pay close attention to this aspect of your display. Don't just throw up a bunch of lights and think that is all there is to it.

Arranging Your Merchandise

For most craftspeople, arranging merchandise on shelves is the job that consumes more time than any other part of the setup ritual. If you're a potter, it may mean removing hundreds of pieces of pottery from their packing crates, unwrapping each piece of work, and finding the proper place for it on your shelves.

A jeweler will spend hours pinning every earring to a board and setting each ring in a case. A booth featuring what we earlier referred to as Foo-Foo may literally involve 500 to 1,000 odds and ends—bits of craft work of every conceivable size. Every floral display must be hung to its best advantage. We—I shouldn't say we—Judy would spend three or fours hours before every show, arranging our baskets, while I disappeared, or stood around looking ineffectual.

There's a critical reason why this part of setup takes so much time: how you display your craft can drastically effect how much you sell. Little decorative touches that enhance the customers' visual pleasure and help to entice them into the booth can make a big difference in your sales. You'll see abundant examples of these kinds of touches in the photographs. Where you strategically place your merchandise is even more important.

To maximize the advertising and selling potential of your booth, your most attractive big sellers should generally be at eye level or below. In that position, customers not only see your craft at close range and from the best vantage point, but they can touch it and pick it up. That tactile possibility inspires customer desire. Eye level or below also enables shorter people to view your craft without having to reach for it. At the same time, women often like to rummage. Some customers are always looking for things that are out of the way, treasures that everybody else missed. With some exceptions, as noted in a few of the photographs, most often a fully stocked booth caters to this customer tendency.

Storage Space

The question of a fully stocked booth leads to the question of just where do you put all this merchandise in so small a space? With the only exception I can think of being jewelers, who can carry $50,000 worth of merchandise in three or four suitcases, the rest of us have to strategically work this problem out.

If you are very clever at arranging space and your particular craft makes it possible, set all your merchandise for your customers to see. However, it may be necessary, to set aside some space—preferably out of sight, behind you, or under tables—where you can keep your extra inventory handy in order to replace stock as it sells. If you are a solo act, as Judy often was, on a busy day you will not have time to leave the booth and go back to your truck, where more merchandise may be stored.

Remember that you want the customer to feel that she has every possible choice. If potential buyers don't see something that is exactly right, you can reach into that handy storehouse and show them something else that may be just what they wanted. Booths using display tables have it easy: Space under the table itself allows for convenient storage. In every photograph in which there is a table, particularly one covered by a tablecloth, you can be sure something is stored underneath. If use of a table is not appropriate to your craft, you will have to find another method of storage.

At most outdoor shows, storage of extra merchandise is rarely a problem. There is usually a good deal of room behind you, and sometimes you'll be able to park your vehicle right behind your booth. At indoor shows, the promoter usually sets aside a large portion of floor space where everybody can store merchandise and quickly retrieve it, as needed. But don't count on it everywhere.

The Advantage of an Open Booth

The presentation of most craft products is best served by providing customers with entry to your booth, so they can come in and browse. Tables or even very narrow entryways generally present a barrier between you and potential buyers and hamper customers' view of merchandise displayed at the back of the booth or behind you. If the aisles are crowded, a potential customer may barely glance into your booth. A few customers standing in front of the table can also block the aisles, making it almost impossible for people to clearly view your product. A booth arranged in this fashion discourages would-be customers. They usually don't want to have to fight to see or enter a booth. Sometimes, when the aisles are jammed as at Christmas shows, the customer will be jostled and shoved right past your booth—like rush hour on the subway—without ever seeing anything.

The scenario above applies to the normal show but, ironically, the opposite effect can occur and work in your favor during the holiday season. If your booth is jammed with people, it often prompts others to check out what all the fuss is about. Human nature being what it is, when people see a large crowd gazing at, examining, and buying your product, they can't help but be intrigued. They will then squeeze, push, and shove their way into the booth to see what they are missing out on and buy something, just because so many others are buying. So spend as much time as is necessary to create a booth arrangement that attracts lots of customers into the booth and then assists you in keeping them there until they buy something.

This is also a time when the height of your booth and shelving is important. If the inventory is moving out fast and the booth is crowded with people, instead of keeping things at eye level, you may find that high shelving works better, because it allows you to stock more inventory. High shelving may pose a problem because some people can't reach products high up without assistance. On the other hand, some people are always intrigued by what is furthest away and hardest to reach. Human nature, I guess.

Price All Your Merchandise

Every item in your booth should have a price tag on it, which is easy to see and read. People do not like to ask you how much a particular item costs. For many people, asking the price is embarrassing. Asking how much something costs automatically implies that you may not be able to afford it. Lack of a price tag, therefore, can cost you a sale.

In addition, when the booth is crowded, the customer may not have the time to wait in line just to ask a price. More important to the psychology of selling, is the fact that when people are shopping they are uncomfortable admitting to you, or even to themselves, that they cannot afford something. Certainly the customer is aware of her finances and her budget, that's why she's looking at the price tag, but she doesn't want to discuss it with you. Absence of a price tag forces her to do so.

Sometimes the absence of a price tag encourages dickering over the price and attempts by the customer to bargain. You should never bargain with the customer.

Demonstrate Your Product

We aren't suggesting that you become a pitchman, modeling yourself after a salesman for a new vegetable slicer or a miracle stain remover. We're still talking about booth arrangement and how to allow the space to make the most of your wares.

Some products speak for themselves: A kite is a kite; a bowl is a bowl. But the uses of other crafts—like our baskets—may be less apparent and may need to be demonstrated. Less traditional products often confuse people. Rather than ask what a product is for and risk appearing stupid or ignorant, they may simply leave the booth.

We realized that this could happen when we fielded repeated questions like, "This is a beautiful basket, but what do I do with it?" Sometimes I was tempted to tell them. But, I remained professional—particularly if my wife was standing next to me. One day however, I couldn't resist. We had made a basket we called a bird basket because it resembled a traditional birdhouse without a roof. We displayed delicate soaps and small towels in it. Still, a woman asked me the question, "What do I do with it?" So I told her to hang it in a tree. Judy didn't think that was very funny. Neither did the lady. I disappeared and Judy mollified her and sold her another basket. I didn't hear the end of that for a while.

Since each of our baskets was designed for a different purpose, they were placed on the shelves with something in them—napkins in a napkin holder, a bottle of wine in a picnic basket, toilet paper in another small basket. Nevertheless, some people were oblivious to the obvious and still asked the question. The bird basket incident happened the last year we were in business, so I guess my patience had run out and it was time to retire.

If your craft is strictly decorative, give it a background that enhances it and shows it off. If it is a hands-on item—a ceramic mixing bowl, perhaps—

place it in the customer's hand. Let her touch it and feel it. Encourage the customer to develop an attachment to it. Try to help the customer relate to the product by discussing her home and where she wants to put it in her home. Point out or refer the customer to those pictures in your album that creatively depict how you use it in your home or yard, or wherever the craft is appropriate.

Learn to play your booth space. The entire booth can be considered an artistic medium or environment in which you work and ply every aspect of your trade. Use your booth space to take your customer on a shopping tour. Get out of your chair and mingle with people. Take things off the shelf and hand them to the customer. "Did you see this? Is this the color you're looking for? Maybe this suits your needs better?" Or just restock and rearrange your merchandise from time to time. By doing that—a seemingly simple, innocent act—you can make customers in your booth take notice, look at your craft more closely, ask questions, and buy. As difficult as it may be, no question a customer asks should ever be ignored or treated as stupid, my occasional sarcasm not withstanding. Instead, as Beth Weber, craftsperson and promoter said, "Remind them that they have creative talents that you don't have." And, I'll add, even if it isn't true.

Most customers enjoy getting to know you. Quite a few, particularly the elderly, attend craft shows out of loneliness. The craft show is their opportunity to get out of the house, be with people, and still feel that they are safe. Many, many of the craftspeople we have met in the business have never considered this factor—most likely because they live in a world only of crafts. They forget that most people do not have the talent or imagination to do what they are doing.

Customers admire and even envy your creative ability; occasionally, they even express those feelings with a comment like, "Oh! I could never do this." That is the time to say what Beth said, reminding them that they probably have talents you do not have. A little flattery goes a long way when selling a product. At the same time, you want—in a modest way, while thanking them for their appreciation of your art—to take advantage of the customer's perspective of you as an artist. In the vernacular, this is called "working the crowd."

Advertise Yourself

At first reading, you are apt to think that there is no way to advertise yourself at a show, and, admittedly, what we are suggesting is subtler than what is traditionally thought of as *advertising*. We are not recommending that you walk the aisles or stand in the entrance, hawking your wares like a carnival barker. Yet there are many ways to self-advertise without upsetting the promoter, irritating customers, or drawing complaints from other craftspeople.

One of the most important ways to advertise is to create a large banner with your business name and logo on it. Many large promotions require such a banner. Hang the banner at the front of your booth, from the top of it, at an angle out over the aisle. Most experienced artisans display such a banner at every show—indoor and outdoor—but particularly at indoor shows. In large shows, crowded with customers, the banner enables the customer to look down long rows of craft booths and spot your booth.

Some top-of-the-line shows like the Harvest Festival may post a directory with a map of the entire floor layout and the name of every craft booth on the map. This is another form of advertising, and it is a real help to customers who are looking for your booth among 500 or 600 competitors. Other promoters, such as Fire on the Mountain, will request that you contribute a piece of your work to be displayed in showcases at the entrance to the show. This is usually optional, but you should definitely take advantage of this form of advertising. Every customer who walks in is going to see a sample of your work without walking up and down the long aisles.

Another technique was one we learned by accident. The technique could be classified as *selling*, but it was also a form of displaying. At one of our earliest shows, our booth space was way off in the back of the show and very few customers were coming our way. I had reason to return a large picnic basket to our truck and was walking through the show, only to have a number of women stop me and ask where I had purchased it. They later showed up at the booth. Thereafter, whenever the buying action seemed slow, or our booth space seemed out of the flow of the crowd, either Judy or I or our young son would amble casually around with a picnic basket in our hand. This won't work for all crafts, but if yours fits the bill, I recommend the technique.

The Perils of Tearing Down

In spite of the chapter title, we would be remiss if we didn't include a few words about teardown—that time when you pack up all your inventory, break down your booth, load it in your truck, and head for home. This can often be the most exasperating and tedious time of the entire show—the most frustrating and absolutely aggravating. Well, you can tell how much I enjoyed it. Judy always displayed the self-control and patience of a saint, while all I wanted to do was get home.

Because you are approaching the closing hour, the time drags. Most of the customers (except a few who think they can find a bargain) have headed home. You would like to follow in their tire tracks and you would like to start clearing the shelves, beginning the sweaty process of leaving the show behind you. After two or three days, you are tired, bedraggled, and want only to shower, sit in your favorite and most comfortable chair, and sip a martini or a brandy or whatever happens to be your beverage preference. However, regardless of what you want, the promoter's rules say closing time is five o'clock or when the beer and wine stops flowing. As we explained, those rules you must follow.

It is at this time that a craft show most resembles a traveling circus and the mood can be summed up as "every man for himself." Maybe a few hundred vehicles are getting ready to line up for a relatively few parking spots. If you're at the end of the line, you may be two to three hours getting out of the show and you realize that, in that time, you could have been home—if you'd been first in line. In every direction you will see other craftspeople heading for their cars and, if you're like me, you want to also. If you are by yourself, you have no choice in the matter, which for me is even more frustrating. It was in that situation that Judy learned self-control. I never did.

This situation provokes a lot of anxiety, and that is why we're taking the time to describe it. At this point, there is a strong temptation to cheat a bit on the promoter's rules on parking or packing up early, and sometimes you may get away with it. I know, because I was always tempted and often tried. Beth Weber always gave us a booth space right across from her—I think, in part, to prevent me from doing it. She let us into the show because she liked Judy and she knew that Judy would restrain me. It's a good thing she did. The end of the show is not the time to clash with the promoter. That promoter will remember you next year and may well reject your application. So be patient—as much as it kills you.

If you are by yourself, use the time to do an inventory. Cash out your register and put your money away safely. That means having a money belt secured tightly around your waist. Then, when it is closing time, take down your booth and wait until it is either possible to pull your truck up to your booth space or you can leisurely begin hauling everything to wherever your vehicle is parked.

Take your time and don't allow yourself to become frustrated. You'll find the drive home more relaxed and a lot safer. We've seen a lot of accidents because frustrated craftspeople were too anxious to get home. Judy backed into one. This is not the way to end a show.

8

Dealing with Customers

THE READER MAY WONDER WHY WE ARE DEVOTING A chapter to this. After all, don't you just collect the money and allow your product to sell itself? The answer is yes, and no, but mostly no. As we have stressed in the previous chapters, the crafts business is a business just like any other. True enough, you may not have a store in which potential customers shop on a regular basis, but for the two or three days that you are doing a craft show, your booth is a store and you should regard it as such. It is very much like owning a chain of stores in a variety of places.

As must be clear by now, I personally am not the salesman type; Judy is. However, I'm not referring to the stereotypical, high-pressure salesman you find in a used-car lot. I'm discussing people who genuinely enjoy people and can spend ten hours a day dealing with them. Judy is that kind of person. Being an optimist, she took the approach that every show would be a great show, even though she knew better. She greeted people from the standpoint that most people are good people and that if you treat them nicely, they will respond in kind. Most of the time she was right.

I tend to be a pessimist, probably because of my background in law enforcement. After the uniqueness of the business wore off, I had to come to terms with the truth that I just didn't enjoy selling—even our creations—for any extended period of time. Judy took pleasure in it. That is why we were so successful.

Be Honest with Each Other and Yourself

As we mentioned in the previous chapter, if you have a partner, you should divide the tasks of the business based on each person's abilities. You will have to decide who is best suited to spend the most time in the booth—based on both knowledge of the product and sales ability. If you are a solo act and selling does not come naturally to you, you'll have to develop a rapport with people, learning to accept each individual for what and who he is, for those few minutes that he spends in your booth. If you are unable to do that, you probably won't make a lot of money and may not be in business long. Making money, no matter how good your product, depends a great deal on how well you relate to the public. However, you don't need special training in salesmanship. What you do need is to apply some common sense to each new situation in which you find yourself.

Spend some time evaluating your own personality and discuss the subject with your partner. If you have a temper, learn to control it. If you tend to be sarcastic, as I do, remember that many people do not appreciate that kind of humor and will react to it as to an insult. If you are the more serious and somber type, learn to smile and expose your personality and sense of humor a little more.

More than anything, keep in mind that people are not in your booth to engage in intellectual dialogue. Some want to chitchat, others are strictly business. Try to learn to recognize the type of individual with whom you are dealing. When the booth is very crowded, it probably won't make a difference, because neither you nor the customer has time for idle conversation. But when customers are scarce, if you are not the kind of person who easily engages in light, pass-the-time-of-day conversation, practice and develop the ability. Just talk a little more, let yourself go. If you tend to talk too much and overwhelm people, learn to listen. More than anything else, be sensitive to the customer. It may mean the difference between keeping a customer in your booth or watching her leave it empty-handed, the difference between a sale and no sale.

Some Absolute Nos and Nevers

Here's a very good example of what we are concerned with here. A young man had the booth next to ours at one of our last Christmas shows. Having watched him for some hours, we noted that he (1) had a very presentable look, and—as I learned after having to force some conversation—(2) was quite intelligent, with an a easygoing personality, when he used it. The wood product he was displaying was of a superior quality. Anyone seeking the product he was offering would have been proud to display his chessboards and other game accessories, but very few potential customers purchased anything from him. Most walked into the booth, took note of his aloof attitude, and walked right out again.

From the moment the show opened Saturday morning until it closed Sunday night, this young man never got out of his chair to greet a customer and he never stopped reading his book. If asked a question, he looked up from his book, perfunctorily answered the question, and returned to his reading. He finished the book by the end of the show, but he made very little money.

Regrettably, it is not uncommon to see many craftspeople doing the same thing at almost any craft show that you attend. If they are not reading a book or doing a crossword puzzle, they are reading the morning newspaper. Would you like or expect to walk into a shopping mall, walk up to the register to make a purchase and find a newspaper acting as a barrier between you and the clerk?

Then there is the craftsperson (sometimes even a friend) who, when things seem slow, comes to your booth, stands in front of the counter, and talks endlessly. Dealing with this can be especially difficult and most experienced craftspeople know better. Maybe it is slow in his booth, but that doesn't mean it is slow in yours. If another merchant is engaging you this way and you see it is interfering with your ability to deal with your customers, just excuse yourself and walk over to a customer. That is a quick way to terminate the conversation and should be understood by any craftsperson with any savvy.

Sure, it is boring to sit in your booth like a caged animal when there are few or no customers. After lunch hours or before closing, patronage is always slow and time does drag. But reading a book is not the way to attract anyone into your booth. With your head in a book, you have no idea who has walked by, or even who may have stepped inside the booth, stepped out again, and continued down the aisle to buy in another booth or from your competitor. There were other chessboards in that show I mentioned.

Judy and I learned along the way that oftentimes the person selling in the next booth is not the person who actually produced the product. I later found out that the dour young man at the Christmas show did not produce the chessboards he was selling; rather, he had been hired by the artisan to sell for him. Sometimes, for personal or business reasons (to be discussed in a later chapter), the craft artists will hire people to go out on the road and sell their products. The young man was a poor example of this. On salary, he had nothing to lose by reading his book. That craftsperson had no idea of how much money he was losing as a result of this man's supercilious attitude and lack of sales ability. That can be a lesson to you if you ever consider hiring someone to do your shows.

For the big craft operations, hiring sales help is no doubt profitable and convenient. Maybe some craftspeople have little to lose, but we don't recommend hiring someone else to sell your craft. There is just too much profit to be lost.

More than once, we agreed to mind a booth for what we believed were fellow craftspeople, only to find out when they returned, hours later, that they were hired personnel who had no emotional or financial investment in the craft. On a straight salary, no commission, these hired hands could care less about tending to business. If for some reason you should have to hire someone, hire carefully and firmly set your rules.

Even sending out family members to sell your merchandise does not guarantee a profitable show. As conscientious and personable as our daughter and son-in-law were when we tried this one year, we found that they just never sold as much as we had sold at the same show for years in the past. If it had happened at only one show, we would have chalked it up to a bad year, but since it occurred at every show they did, we had to attribute it to some intangible personality factors and just plain experience. Perhaps nobody can have the same devotion to a product as the person who has sweated blood to produce and perfect it.

Yet, on rare occasions and under special circumstances, assisting a fellow craftsperson can be rewarding. One day, a neighboring craftswoman, whom Judy had never met before, had vehicle problems that had to be resolved if she was to get home. This required her to leave the booth for more than three hours. Judy hung a sign on her booth referring customers to our booth and managed both. Sales in both booths were excellent and the woman gave Judy a very nice gift from her best wares. We have developed a close friendship since that day. That was a rare occurrence and we still don't recommend doing this very often.

There is a tendency among craftspeople—usually when business is slow—to leave their booths unattended and walk the show themselves, stopping to talk to a dozen friends along the way, generally about how bad the show is. How would they know why it was bad, when they were never in their booth to improve their sales?

On many occasions, we have been next to merchants who had the nerve to ask us to "mind their booth for a moment" and then were gone for hours. We learned to never, never be talked into this, unless there were very extenuating circumstances. Certainly help out if a neighbor has to make a rush call to the bathroom or wants to quickly get something to drink, but you don't want to be stuck trying to conduct their business as well as your own, keeping track of money transactions for them, while tending to your own. In that case, your business will inevitably suffer. You must focus on and be concerned about the people entering your booth; you can't be distracted by what is happening in the unattended booth next to you. Customers know that they can walk down the aisle and find something they like someplace else.

That doesn't mean that you attack the customer like a vulture on a rabbit. All that is required is that you look as interested in the customer as you want her to be in your product—and you have to be in the booth to do that. Have a smile on your face. Acknowledge the customer with some sort of a greeting. You might ask if she needs any help, but we caution you that there is some risk in opening a conversation with that old refrain. If the customer says no, and she often will, you are left out on a nonconversational limb. So try to be versatile. Skip clichés like, "Oh what a beautiful morning." Maybe ask if she's enjoying the show.

That's more general and less apparently pushy. Most of all, keep your mind fixed on the fact that this is now your livelihood and no longer a hobby.

We couldn't guess at how much money we have seen lost because a craftsperson had a haughty attitude or conducted business in the absentee manner described above. Hundreds of times we told a neighbor, "You had a customer who said they'd be back." Well, you know about the "Be Back Family." Guess how many ever returned? You shouldn't have to concern yourself with the potential customers entering another booth.

The Positive Approach and Techniques You Can Use

When customers have stepped across that imaginary line we spoke of earlier, most of them are in the booth because they are considering spending their money on your product. It is at that moment that you should remember that you are dependent on them, not the other way around. If you are truly financially independent of the customer, I don't know why you would be out working in this marketplace at all.

Most craftspersons are sensitive to people and, with some experience, you will find that you can sense what approach is needed. Some people want absolutely no conversation, while others would stand at your counter and talk all day. To customers who don't want to chitchat, just explain your product and let them do the rest. With very talkative customers, if you are not busy, indulge them. If you are getting busy, develop a way of cutting short your conversation without being impolite. Excuse yourself and explain that another customer needs you. This I found easy and Judy found more difficult.

If the customer seems to be in a dilemma and you suspect she is concerned about price, subtly, without ever mentioning cost, show her something less expensive. Basically, just engage her in the same sort of normal, friendly conversation you would a person in any other circumstance. Try to exude enthusiasm and pride in your product. That generates interest and appreciation, which, in turn, generates sales.

Judy was very adept at complimenting people and she did it genuinely. She would observe them and instinctively find some nice, friendly way to greet them. She might comment on a woman's blouse or earrings or sweater or hair. If the woman was pregnant, she would ask when she was expecting. If children were brought into the booth, she reacted to them positively.

When it came to children strolling around our booth, especially if their parents didn't have them on a leash, I usually worried a lot. Watching a child poke into every basket, I'd sit there fretting about when the kid was going to drop ice cream or a Slurpy or a hot dog into one of them. Since this type of accident only happened once in seventeen years, obviously, I was worrying about a remote possibility. I just had more difficulty adjusting to potentially adverse circumstances. Through the years, my concerns about the prospect of children wreaking havoc on our booth abated, particularly as I noted that more than one child—especially little girls who are learning to shop—showed their mother an item that the mother later purchased.

Occasionally, you'll get some breakage and damage may be done, but that happens to every store owner. It is part of the business, so learn to accept it; otherwise, you'll become a nervous wreck, as I was in the beginning and for quite a few years thereafter. You can purchase liability insurance, but insurance companies who handle this business are hard to find and unless you are dealing in very expensive and easily breakable merchandise, the cost may not be worth it. Because an underwriter's estimate of cost would vary so drastically, depending on your product and the expense involved in developing your booth, you will need to investigate this and make a decision that is relevant to your unique product and circumstances.

Stand Behind Your Product

How many times in your life have you made a purchase, brought it home, and found that it was defective? And how many times have you found that, for a variety of reasons, you either could not return it to the store from which it was purchased or you could not get your money back or a replacement? If this has happened to you, you know that you probably never purchased anything from that store again.

As a merchant and as an artist, you must be always ready to stand behind your product if you want to maintain good customer relations and a repeat customer business. In our case, if a customer found a minor defect in a basket, but still wanted to purchase it, we would discount the price. If the customer wanted that particular style of basket with identical fabric and we didn't have one in stock at the show, we would make another especially for her without adding the shipping cost. On the rare occasion that something a customer purchased broke when she got it home, we asked no questions and simply sent her another basket. Sure, maybe once or twice it was a flimflam job, but far more often, the customer respected our integrity and came back to buy many times in the future.

Appeal to the Customer's Senses and Sense of Self-Importance

Suppose you notice a customer ogling your product, but the customer seems wary about touching it. Put it in her hand. As a promoter said to me when discussing the jury process, "Handmade crafts and original art, need to be seen, touched, and, in some cases, even the fragrance needs to be experienced." Psychologically, it's harder for a customer to resist buying something after she has applied her senses to it. Then, while she is holding it, help her picture it on her or in her home or wherever your product is appropriate. If you're selling something wearable, wear it yourself. If it is decorative, tell customers where you place it in your home.

If it's important to selling your craft, have a mirror in your booth. That small album hanging in your booth, with photographs of the product in various settings, is also helpful. And, if you don't have what the customer really wants, be honest about it and refer her to some other craft booth where she may find it. I can't tell you how many times just exhibiting that little bit of honesty later brought the customer back to our booth.

Don't assume that every person has the ability to envision your product in use, or in the appropriate setting. Ask whether the customer is buying for herself or someone else. Is it a gift? What's the special occasion? If it is a gift, refresh her memory as to her friend's favorite colors or help her mentally reconstruct her friend's house or even her personality. Some people have great imaginations; others don't. Taking the time and effort to give the customer this kind of personal attention lets her know that you feel she is important and that you appreciate her interest in your product. We all like that feeling when we walk into a store. One of my biggest gripes is walking all over a department store, unable to find anyone who cares enough about my business to answer a question or help me find what I am looking for.

Though I wasn't at ease with this approach at first, I did learn to do these things and found that I began to enjoy the response I received. I never could get myself to say "What a beautiful baby" when the kid was ugly, but if you want to keep some mother in your booth while she is shopping and trying to manage three kids at the same time, be ready and prepared to help her out. We kept some candy in the booth for children. Before you give candy to their kids, always ask the parents for their permission first. Buy a string of stamps and put one on a child's hand. Engage them in conversation about it.

Maybe you can keep the children amused. Have some small games in the booth or children's reading material or coloring books. If you have room in back of your booth, as at some outdoor shows, invite the children to sit down back there while their mother shops (always checking with the mother first, of course). If the mother is pushing a stroller, invite her to roll it to the back of your booth so it doesn't block all your booth space. We had triplets in the booth one day and that stroller left no room for anybody else.

The main point is that each potential customer is really just a new person you are meeting for the first time. If meeting people isn't natural to you, you'll find that it becomes more natural after a number of shows. Any initial reticence or shyness or sense that you're being phony disappears with experience. Maybe it is as simple as "Do unto others." The rest will come naturally. Your customers will feel important and respected.

Keep in mind that the customer coming to a craft show is there for a good time. It is an event to which she was looking forward. You're simply part of that event and it is your job to help her have as good a time as possible. Maybe she won't buy from you that moment and you'll think you've wasted your time, but you'll be surprised to find how many come back a few hours later and purchase from you just because you made her time in your booth pleasurable. I was stunned at how many of our longtime customers came over to us, gave us a big hug at our last show, and told us how much they were going to miss us.

People come to craft shows for many reasons. Some are looking for entertainment or people around them. Others want to get out of the house for the day, to give their kids and the dog a walk, and so on. You'll see a lot of people just out for a bicycle ride. Compared to other forms of entertainment, the craft show is an inexpensive outing. The more enjoyable you make it for them, the more money you are also likely to make for yourself. This may seem like nothing more than common sense, but putting it into action isn't always easy.

As a probation officer, by nature and training I was a pretty cynical person. The kind of interpersonal skills necessary to sell are hardly the same ones needed in dealing with criminals. Yet, little by little, as I relaxed, I also began to like people more. We suggest that you try to cultivate this type of people-friendly attitude if you want to be a success. If I could do it, anybody can.

Men at a Craft Show

There is one group of people with whom you will deal regularly, who require a few words that may seem to contradict everything that has been advised up to this point. Men—particularly husbands—can pose the biggest threat to your sales. A husband can take more business away than your fiercest competitor. No one we know ever really solved this problem.

Long before I got into the crafts business, I was a typical husband. Judy had to drag me to a craft show. You'll see countless men in this position. The husband does not want to be at the show and is simply patronizing and indulging his wife. This husband takes the kids along and pretends it's a family day out, but he really wants to be home watching the football game and is not inclined to spend money on crafts.

Since it may not be fair to apply what I just said to all men, I'll modify my opinion to this extent: Some promoters have noticed an increasing number of men attending craft shows held in new markets. It is speculated that this may be the result of the increasing number of women now in the workplace and on different work schedules. As a result, perhaps the craft show is beginning to truly represent an entertaining day out with the family.

Having stated this caveat, I'm still not convinced that this trend represents the majority of men, dutifully tagging along behind their wives at craft shows.

What I observed for seventeen years was that as the wife enters your booth, the husband gently eases her out. Every item she picks up, he finds fault with. "We don't need it. What are you going to do with it? Where can you possibly put it? I can make it myself." That verbal reaction is almost as predictable as the sun rising. This is why Saturdays are generally better financially than Sundays. On Saturday, most women attend a craft fair alone or with a female friend, and they are there to shop and buy.

On most Sundays, particularly during the summer months, the show is crowded with young people who have no money or husbands who have no interest in being there. Ironically, let a husband who truly wants to buy his wife something enter the booth, and inevitably she'll talk him out of the purchase. She is going to demonstrate her frugality. Dare I say, that is typically female, or am I engaging in stereotyping or male chauvinism?

Whatever! That's life, I guess. Conversely, the nice young couples who stroll by and who are either engaged to be married or have just begun dating, act quite differently. The young man wants to make an impression. He is always ready to open his wallet. The love of his life at the moment can have almost anything that she wants. That is certainly typically male and I'd bet no women objects to that kind of stereotyping.

We found that the best response to the husband's negativity is to be as cordial as possible and even agree with his negative attitude. I would commiserate with him and tell him about how I once felt about craft shows before I got into the business. I'd talk sports with him or politics or anything to distract him from his wife's involvement with our baskets. Meanwhile, Judy would be engaging the wife in craft conversation, showing her various baskets, their use and differing prices.

Sometimes reverse psychology generates a sale. Be truthful and admit that you know they don't "need" your product. In reality, there is nothing for sale at a craft show that any of us can't live without. Acknowledge that your product is an extravagance that not everyone can afford. Husbands don't like to admit that they can't afford something. Depending on how I sized up the man, I might also suggest how sometimes it is necessary to indulge a wife, pointing out how it is better than having her upset. Then, when he realized that his wife really wanted a basket, he usually opened his wallet, if not truly his heart.

One good selling technique is to point out that only at craft shows can such items be found at such a reasonable price. On the side, I would suggest to the husband that if his wife really wanted a basket, he might be better off buying it at a craft show, than have her buying it at Macy's. If the man had remarked that he could make it himself, I would engage him in a conversation about woodworking, ask about how much he did, what kind of equipment he had, and how much time and money he thought it would require to make just one basket. Most often, that would discourage him and he'd approve of his wife spending $48.

However, if none of that worked, we'd thank them for their interest and I'd wish the man luck making the basket. Many times, an hour or so later, the wife would come back and purchase the basket with the words, "He'll never make me the damn basket." Beyond that, just graciously thank them for stopping by and looking. You've done all you can and the purchase is up to them. Remember the adage, "The customer is always right." Without customers, you have no business.

Controlling Your Own Feelings

As in other endeavors, there will be days when you don't want to be at a craft show. Some days you may not feel well; other days you're just not in the mood; still other days, you may have other problems distracting your attention. On days when everything irritates you, you really won't want to see another human being, much less talk to one. I had a lot of days like that and, when I did, Judy gave me the signal to disappear. There will be days when any of the foibles and weaknesses to which we are all prone, will be affecting you. When that happens, remember how you feel and what you expect when you enter any store as a buyer. The customer is not interested in your problems; she has enough of her own. So, on those bad days, just dig down deep and get through the day. The show must go on.

9

An Overview of the Crafts Business—and Beyond

S JUDY AND I REVIEWED THIS BOOK, WE RECOGNIZED that there were numerous aspects of the crafts business that did not fit into any categories we had previously covered. Still, we wanted you to be aware of them, because they are pertinent to your business and your future.

Wholesaling Your Product

As you conduct your business, you may be approached in person at a show or by telephone by people inviting you to display your merchandise in their boutique. They may offer to buy your product—at a wholesale price—for sale in their shop.

As you consider this proposition, the natural inclination is to consider the offer a wonderful opportunity to sell more of your craft and make more money. There is good money to be made in these markets. Many craftspeople manufacture their craft exclusively for this kind of market. Others supplement their show income through this kind of outlet. But before making a quick decision about wholesaling your craft, many factors should be seriously considered.

Manufacturing for such marketplaces and maintaining your production schedule become exceptionally labor-intensive and pressure-packed, particularly with a heavy show lineup. This fact is often forgotten when the offer is particularly tempting. You can easily jump to the conclusion that you've discovered a quick source of additional income. For exactly those reasons, we succumbed to these invitations early in our career. We learned—not quickly enough—that all too frequently our profits dwindled and the enterprise became more trouble, work, and aggravation than it was worth.

When you consider selling wholesale, you can opt for one of four basic types of business arrangements. The first and most preferable is a straight sale to the shop owner. The shop owner wants a wholesale price and intends to purchase some specified quantity of your product. This shop owner's intent is to double the price in his store. He wants a wholesale price from you that will allow him to generate a substantial profit without having to charge a price that discourages customers. Because he is ordering in volume, the owner will try to convince you that he deserves this hefty discount. On the surface, this seems reasonable and what really attracts your attention is the big check the shop owner will immediately write.

However, the financial fact of life is that, at a craft show, you are already selling at a wholesale price. That is why you don't discount your product at a show for any reason. A craftsperson's biggest drawing card is that people buy at shows because they are not paying shopping mall prices. What you must determine, before you accept this proposition, is how much further your price can be reduced and still compensate you for the materials and labor invested. Your price is probably at that bottom line already!

If you estimate that this wholesale price renders a reasonable profit, you may want to make the deal. Don't do so, however, without first factoring in the time involved to produce more product and how that time is spent, which may or may not detract from the time you need to produce pieces for your craft shows.

Having considered that, if you are confident that you can profitably keep up with this addition to your workload, make the deal. When you do, get the order in writing, set a delivery date, and request some upfront money—if not the full price, at least a down payment, with the remainder to be paid on delivery. If you don't do this, you have no guarantees that the shop owner will still want your merchandise when you deliver it. The shop could even cease to exist by the delivery date. This amounts to conducting your business professionally.

About three years into our business, we were approached by two restaurant owners who wanted a large number of customized napkin holders for their establishment. The number made it worthwhile to sell to them at an agreed-on wholesale price. This was a one-time-only deal and netted us a nice profit without too much extra work.

Making a wholesale agreement with a shop or boutique owner can, however, involve many other problems. If the shop owner has a successful business and your items are selling well, the owner will probably continue to order from you until sales diminish and your items are taking up shelf space from pieces that are selling better than yours. If you can supply one or more stores and still maintain your inventory for shows, there is no reason *not* to engage in this business. When deciding on a wholesale price, you must be sure to factor in the cost of shipping your items and picking up your merchandise when your product is no longer desired.

In rare cases, the proprietor may request that you refrain from doing a show in the vicinity of his store. The shop may be open during the craft show, so the owner is not happy about the competition. From the owner's standpoint, his shelf price for your product is going to be much higher than your price at the craft show. Thus, in doing a show in the owner's community, you are underselling your own product at that store and undermining the shop owner's price.

Renting Floor Space in a Shop

You may be confronted with a proposal from a store owner who will rent you floor space, space in which you will set up a permanent booth to display your craft. This arrangement seemed intriguing, so we did it twice and encountered every negative this business arrangement presents.

In reality, the proprietor is simply creating a perpetual craft show, a mini-fair. Your rental fees are more than paying all the proprietor's bills. Furthermore, he expects to receive perhaps 10 percent of your gross sales each month, adding to his profit and subtracting from yours. That may require you to raise your price to compensate and may therefore render your craft less attractive to customers.

In these situations, nothing is provided but the floor space. You incur the expense of creating an attractive minibooth and keeping it well stocked each month. That means additional travel or shipping expense. The proprietor only has to sit by the cash register and collect the money. You price tag each item, so there is no commingling of funds and you must keep an accurate record of inventory that is now out of your control, sitting in one or more shops. It also behooves you to verify what and how much was sold, how much money you are owed, and what you have to replace. Meanwhile, that unsold inventory, sitting in that boutique, is not accessible to you should you need it at a show.

As the manufacturer, you may now be adding substantially to your production volume, while much of your merchandise is not generating any income. As the months pass, you will discover the inevitable: The shop exists as a fixed part of the community. It does not have the customer volume of a craft show. The local citizenry who shop there view it as a gift shop. Initially, you'll sell well when your product is new. Later, sales will diminish drastically when regular customers have seen all your merchandise.

Most contracts of this kind are for a minimum of three months. During the holiday season, if you have the right product, this arrangement might be very profitable. But, overall, the proprietor has no personal investment in your craft and knows nothing about its manufacturer. At shows, you are interacting with the customer, discussing your product. Not so in such shops! Your craft is just another drawing card and has to sell itself. The owner wants your craft to sell well so he earns a greater percentage, but he cannot be selling your product and manning the cash register at the same time. Yours is just one of many booths and yours may go a-begging. Eventually, you'll find yourself removing your booth and severing ties with the shop owner, who now has to induce another gullible person to proceed with this arrangement, which pays the proprietor's bills.

Selling on Consignment

We suffered this third business arrangement and its consequences when we accepted an invitation to place our picnic baskets on consignment in an exclusive gift shop in Carmel, California. The proprietor convinced us that he could sell them at double the price, which at that time meant a price tag of $90. In this case, again, the shop owner was not risking his own money. We were invited to use some of the floor and shelf space in the shop. The owner took a percentage of the price we put on the product. His suggested price was just too tempting to refuse.

On an agreed-on date, we delivered six picnic baskets to the shop. The owner then arranged them on a beautiful oak table, set in a huge French window, open to public view. We left enthralled. Five months later, a total of one basket had been sold. When we drove 200 miles to the shop to retrieve the remaining five, we found them not in the shop's window, but on the floor at the back of the store. Naturally, we terminated the agreement, picked up our baskets, and sold them that weekend at our next show. Even in Carmel, California, the price was too high.

Yet, we again succumbed to temptation and agreed to place our baskets with another boutique owner who also graciously agreed to display our craft on consignment. This was not the minifair-type store I described earlier, or the small, exclusive shop. This was a very large, elegant, and beautifully appointed boutique. It was charming, warm, colorful, and especially inviting to women. Like so many boutiques of its kind, it was owned by a woman who had always wanted to own a boutique.

When you agree to this type of deal, you have no input as to where or how your product will be displayed. The proprietor attempts to create a hodgepodge of every conceivable craft through which customers can roam and spend a few hours, if they choose. This proprietor accepts only a small quantity of your merchandise to add to the mix. It will be scattered everywhere around the store. You don't pay for the space. You do set the price. Every negative specified above applies to this arrangement, plus many more.

With apologies to the majority who run such businesses in a professional manner, those who don't can cause you many problems. They also have no personal investment in your craft. Their goal is to fill their floor space to overflowing. If they don't sell your merchandise, they'll sell somebody else's.

Under these conditions, inexperienced proprietors really don't know what and whose inventory they have at any given moment. They have even less idea of how to keep track of it. From delivery time to the store until the next time you drop by, your merchandise will have been handled, manhandled, and moved all over the shop. Visit the store a week later and you may have difficulty even finding your merchandise. Most often, it won't be displayed to the product's best advantage. I'd find our baskets in some corner where a customer had left them or filled to overflowing with some other craft product. Frequently, merchandise was damaged.

Worst of all, some proprietors have absolutely no business sense. A boutique can be as much a hobby, or avocation, as anything else. When it is time to send you your monthly check, you may get a phone call informing you that expenses were really high last month and the payment will be delayed. In one instance, the proprietor didn't even know what she had sold or how much she owed us.

That said, it is not our intention to demean businesses of this type that operate efficiently. Most do! If you wish to market your craft in this manner, as many craftspeople do, you may earn a fairly good living. Just be aware of the problems involved, particularly if you are also trying to keep up with a full craft show schedule.

The Rep or Middle Man

The fourth proposal you may receive comes from a person who will offer to be your "sales representative." This person is a professional, who knows her business, and she may be offering you a wonderful opportunity. But be sure to consider all the ramifications carefully and fully understand the contractual agreement you will be making.

In this case, the representative will take samples of your merchandise to the large trade shows held in cities like New York, Chicago, and Los Angeles. Your product will be displayed to buyers from all over the United States. If a buyer likes your product and believes it will sell in his store, he will submit his orders and set a delivery date. Obviously, your representative takes a percentage.

However, these are not small orders. It could even be Macy's that wants to sell your work and may order 500 of this or 10,000 of that. So be aware of what you are getting yourself into. You are now in the manufacturing business. You must be prepared to manufacture in volume and provide delivery on the agreed-on delivery date. Furthermore, your representative may enter into "tentative sales agreements," whereby the buyer can cancel the order without penalty months after it was taken. You may be stuck with a huge inventory and outlay of money, which you can ill afford. On the positive side, you could, like Rosie, a good friend of ours, get out of the crafts business per se, and now be designing for and managing a large industry, making huge amounts of money—or losing it. You'll hear about Rosie's story later.

More Unusual Methods of Selling Your Craft

Beyond the major sources of income discussed above, two other areas deserve consideration. The first, the catalogue, has existed since the printing press. Selling by catalogue can produce an income, but placing your products in someone else's catalogue is costly, and if you have a large variety of wares, it is difficult and expensive to display them all. Some catalogue producers will accept your photos; others include photographing your product as part of the primary contract. You then must ship your product to the company, so that professional product photographers do the work.

The major problem with selling through a catalogue is that you never know what will be ordered, when, and how much. Some catalogues are published semi-annually, some only annually. If you decide to try this, we suggest that you select one or two of the most outstanding catalogues and be prepared to produce and ship in volume. Again, this can shift the emphasis in your crafts business to manufacturing only, with no time to spend at craft shows. Therefore, some people produce for this market only. The cost of advertising and photography is probably a great deal less than the money invested in producing for shows. We can give you no firsthand advice regarding this enterprise. So if this option is one you think you might prefer, look into the possibilities. Like everything else in the business, it is a gamble and it depends on just how much profit you can live with.

One disadvantage is obvious. You cannot estimate your potential income for the coming year, since you cannot predict the marketability of your product. Crafts are a luxury, often influenced by seasonal changes. How reliable a source of income they may be in this marketplace is questionable. The few people we have met who tried this market gave it up. Even if you're successful, you run into the same pitfalls as you do in dealing with a sales representative.

The Television Market

Anyone who spends time watching television, and has cable or satellite capability, has some idea about how many shopping networks are on television today. This is a huge marketplace with a jury system far removed from the craft show jury. We know one person who tried the Home Shopping Network and, for her, it was a mixed blessing. Her story is worth telling, should you wish to market your crafts this way.

A few years ago, Rosie Lamar, who produces a line of unique stuffed bears, decided to sell her bears through the Home Shopping Network. To do so, she first had to travel to Florida to jury her bears in person. The process was simple. The Home Shopping Network officials liked Rosie's bear. Their experts appraised it and determined that they would have to price the bear at $199. They ordered 250 bears and took 60 percent of the retail price. As a general rule, because of the volume of merchandise they sell and the time element essential to their financial success, they must sell $6,000 worth of merchandise a minute.

Since she was paid for all 250 bears, whether the Home Shopping Network sold them or not, it would seem that Rosie did well, making $79.60 on every bear. However, Rosie had to incur the expense of making a video about how she manufactured the bear. Then she had to hire people to help her complete the order. Rosie had already scheduled her shows. So she now had the added pressure of completing the Home Shopping Network order on time, while trying to conduct her normal, craft show routine. Of course, her craft show schedule suffered a loss of profits.

From her share of the profit, Rosie also bore a number of expenses: She had to cover the cost of purchasing the prescribed stuffing for the bears and the cost of designing boxes to exact specifications to ship the bears. She had to order special shrink-wrap packaging in which to place each bear. All 250 bears had to be shipped to the Home Shopping Network in one shipment, so she had to have special wooden palates constructed—so many boxes to a palate—to add to her cost of shipping. She made some profit but considered the entire experience a disaster. And remember! It was a one-time-only deal, since the Home Shopping Network doesn't often repeat its items.

This cautionary tale doesn't mean that selling via TV isn't a viable and profitable way to market your product. No doubt it is, or so many thousands of products wouldn't be sold in this manner. We can only tell you what Rosie experienced selling her stuffed bears using this marketing venue. Part of the problem was not knowing what to expect ahead of time. She may go through the whole process again with a new design. This time with her eyes wide open!

The Internet

The last category to explore may become—if it hasn't already—*the* way for craftspeople to sell their products. Five years ago, Judy and I very briefly explored the possibility of marketing our baskets on Internet craft markets. It did not seem a worthwhile enterprise to undertake. Marketing over the Internet was still in its infancy and seemed a tenuous enterprise at best.

At that time, I only found a few Web sites devoted to crafts. Yet, what existed was enough to predict that, with expanding technology, it had a future.

That my prediction greatly understated the future of Internet craft sales is obvious. Today you only have to go online and type in "crafter" or "crafting" or variations such as "craft worlds," followed by the name of your state. You could spend a week researching the responses. The number of individuals, shops, and crafts at your fingertips for viewing and purchasing seems endless.

The Internet offers the craftsperson seemingly infinite possibilities, down what are apparently two major avenues. If you have the computer skills, you can create your own Web site; if not, you can either hire a technician to create one for you or you can contract with a company already on the Web and sell your craft online. Some of the largest companies are much like promoters to whom you will ship your product for display in their online shops or giant, virtual craft fairs. Others resemble catalogue selling, except that now it is on the Internet, rather than in a magazine.

The Internet as a market for your product and a means of selling your craft is now an international enterprise of multibillion dollar proportions. Never having sold this way, Judy and I cannot evaluate this avenue from our own experience. We have discussed it with people who are selling this way, and many of the same gambles exist in this market, with a few new twists.

When you create your own Web site, you have no idea how many hits you will receive; that is, people who actually see your Web site—much less order from it. No one may ever find your Web site unless you advertise it on other Web sites or list it with major search engines, both of which cost money. Placing your product on an already established Web site eliminates the need for you to do your own advertising, since these sites—much like promoters— are doing the legwork for you, establishing the Web links, giving you time to produce. But you also have more competition. With your own Web site, your orders would come directly from the customer to you; by working through another Web site, you're involving a middleman, at whatever cost. If you're computer-phobic, like me, selling on the Web may be completely untenable. I panic whenever a warning sign appears. I can't wait to finish this book because I'm afraid the computer will crash before I get all these words onto a disk. But if you are part of the computer generation, here are just a few samples of the possibilities open to you, if you wish to explore this new Internet craft arena.

In just a few short minutes, I quickly found these examples of what is out there:

The Crafters Den, *www.craftersden.com.*, is based in Hudson, New York. This site features dolls, country art, jewelry, baskets, and carpets. An order form can be downloaded, you can order directly over the Net, or you can order through a toll-free telephone number.

Then there is ecraftUSA, *www.ecraftUSA.com*. This site carries the merchandise of a number of vendors who specialize in jewelry, pottery, baskets, apparel, and so on. Consumers can search for items in a variety of ways—by category, by vendor, by material, and the like. Crafters who want to sell their products can find out how to become vendors.

Sign-crafters.com is a company selling panel signs, logo designs, banners, and personalized redwood name signs for your house. You'll see somebody carving out these things at many outdoor craft shows. From the illustrations provided, you can order to your specific design requirements.

In all three instances cited above, these are companies catering to customers who, in the past, sought and found these items exclusively at craft shows.

Another craft marketplace on the Internet is called Sherlon's Virtual Arts and Crafts Mall, *www.sherlonscraftsmall.com*. This site takes you to shops containing every conceivable craft. You simply click on the shop, select the desired item, fill out the order form, and the order goes directly to the craftsperson who produces that product. The crafter fills the order and ships it to you. There is a sign-up form for any craft artist who wishes to display and sell her craft in this online shopping mall.

The last example is a huge craft outlet in Canada called Crafter's Marketplace, *www.crafters@crafter.ca/*. At the time of this writing, there were some twenty-five huge outlet stores spread across Canada featuring only craft products. Crafters set up their booths in one or in every store, then ship their merchandise directly to the store or to a shipping outlet provided by the Marketplace, which then transports it from the outlet to the individual marketplaces. The craft's creator need never spend time in a booth or ever see it for that matter.

This is a large-scale version of the minifair described earlier, existing simultaneously on the Internet and in physical reality. I have no doubt that this concept will someday spread into the United States or some American firm will create a similar enterprise. Maybe it already exists and I just haven't found it. Obviously, you must have a large manufacturing capability to work with an outfit like this. It was not possible for a two-person operation like The Three Basketeers.

At the other end of the spectrum is a Web site called Smokey Mountain Craft Mall, *www.crafternet.com*, based in western North Carolina. If you are just making a few crafts for a hobby and are looking for crafting tips, craft books, or magazines, this is the place to find them. This site also offers links to many other craft sites.

Judging from the Internet's amazing growth in just a few years, it is not surprising that this has become a wide-open market. It is no longer completely virgin territory and only you can determine if you want to join the many explorers taking this new gamble. But what else is a craftsperson, if not an explorer of new territory?

However, in discussing the subject with an expert, we learned that to have a professional build your Web site, you can anticipate a minimal cost of $1,000 for the most basic, entry-level, four-page site. But this would not really put you in business on the Web. Most people believe that to get the most viewers (hits), their Web site must be linked to the major search engines.

Whether this is true, we cannot say, but certain facts are not in dispute. Major search engines give your site exposure to millions of viewers and the linking costs big money. Just to build a Web site capable of transacting business, taking credit card information, providing security for that information, and linking that to a service that checks a person's credit rating would cost thousands of dollars.

If we were beginning our career, Judy and I would cautiously take the gamble and explore this new online craft environment. But this might be a quirk of our personalities, not necessarily yours. The potential rewards are too big to be ignored—if you have the right product.

We must caution you, though, that two promoters with whom we discussed the subject of Internet sales both said that they knew of no one who has really been successful selling this way. That doesn't mean that no one is succeeding, only that these two people weren't aware of anyone who had made a success on the Internet. At the moment, that is a cliché concerning Web businesses in general: Everybody is rushing to start one, and none of them are turning a profit—yet. Once again, it is a gamble. Certainly, it is not an arena in which rank beginners should engage until they have developed a well-tested, successful product. Furthermore, Internet sales eliminates the personal contact with people that many craftspeople enjoy the most.

The major problem that the Internet and any of the ventures, adventures, or misadventures noted above presents seems to stem from the same roots. When yours is a small business, you need to maintain tight control over your inventory and production schedule. The more diversified you become, the more complex become the problems you face in dealing with supply and demand. Selling via catalogue, a sales representative, or the Internet each represents a drastic departure from selling at craft shows. If you are entertaining any of the above options, a cottage industry is probably what you will have to become.

The End of the Craft Road or Taking a New Direction?

About five years ago, The Three Basketeers reached the stage where we were making all the money we could possibly make doing craft shows. We could not produce any more baskets and we could not participate in any more shows.

We had reached a financial stone wall. We had maximized our output, we faced rising costs, and our profit was diminishing. In essence, we could not supply any greater demand. The options open to us were scary.

When and if you run into this scenario, your choices are three. You can work yourself into a mental frenzy and maybe a hospital. You can retire, as we did, or you can develop a small manufacturing concern, sometimes referred to as a cottage industry. Had we been twenty years younger, we would have chosen the cottage industry option, and possibly have become very wealthy. But to start a cottage industry is a very complex process. We were too old and simply lacked the energy and the motivation to undertake a project of this magnitude. We chose to take our savings, wisely invested through the years, and retire to our four acres in Smartville. But we can give you some idea about what is involved in such an enterprise, if you still have the youth and energy.

What Might Have Been

Once upon a time, in an America that existed just a few short decades ago, establishing a cottage industry would have been a relatively simple process. When we first considered the prospect, we thought in those terms. We had the acreage on which to build a separate, modest facility to manufacture in large volume, and we had the money to equip it.

Among our friends throughout the area, there were many men and women in the senior age category and many handicapped people who were extremely capable and readily available to work. They desperately wanted to work with their hands and hearts and brains again, on a part-time or full-time basis, to supplement the income they received from Social Security, disability, or retirement. Many just liked the idea of being creative again.

With that in mind, Judy and I developed an expansion plan and had a number of people ready to go to work. Some wanted to work in the manufacture of baskets, others were prepared to take units on the road to sell—either on a straight salary basis or on the more motivational, commission basis. In California, Nevada, and Oregon alone, we could have sent units to two or three shows almost every weekend of the year. Judy and I would have supervised the manufacturing process, scheduled shows, and managed all the necessary business arrangements.

The initial capital outlay was fairly expensive, but we had some money available. We estimated that an investment of about $100,000 would cover the initial building, additional vehicles, and equipment necessary to begin production. If any financing was required, we felt we could easily borrow through a bank loan, venture capitalists, or small-business funding programs.

Thinking we were ready to go beyond the craft show routine, we then discussed this new business venture with our best friend, who was an attorney.

Fred smiled sardonically and patiently explained reality to us. That was when our idea came to a very disappointing, grinding halt.

Fred first pointed out that we needed to establish a corporation. That legal process would cost about $2,000 then—maybe more now—and Fred wasn't charging the fee that another attorney would have assessed.

That wasn't a major stumbling block, but we had neglected to consider a great many other factors. We would have to carry liability and health and unemployment insurance for our employees. Then there was workmen's compensation and disability insurance. I said, "Fred, they're not interested in all of that. They just want to work, keep busy, and make some extra money." Fred laughed and pointed out that it didn't matter what they wanted; what mattered was what the law now required. Of course, the building in which we would be manufacturing would have to be insured for fire and theft, and have the required facilities for the handicapped, including the required number of bathrooms. Each vehicle would have to be fully insured under our corporate name.

Next, Fred raised the question of zoning where we lived. Our acreage is zoned as agricultural. Without special dispensation from the county planning commission, we would have to build in an area that was zoned commercial. That meant purchasing land, in our area, no less than $25,000 an acre and more like $50,000. Of course, building could not begin without the proper permits and having the required environmental impact studies done and approved. That would take time and who knows how much money to meet whatever federal and state requirements were mandated, not to mention potential legal battles should any temporary injunctions be imposed by a court, pending the outcome of disputed issues.

It also became obvious that we were going to need to hire a full-time accountant and tax consultant. Judy had done our books and tax work, but she was not capable of handling accounting, payroll, and taxes on this level. What we had envisioned as "just supervising" a business in which we were experienced, had now turned into an enterprise well beyond our capacity and expertise to administer.

It is a shame that the federal bureaucracy has so intruded in the free enterprise system that it dissuades and discourages so many small entrepreneurs from investing further. In speaking with promoters, we learned that they were unanimous in seeing a decreasing number of young people entering the business and expanding—due, in no small part, to the increasing complexities and repercussions now involved.

These regulations and bureaucratic boondoggles are a factor in the crafts business, as in any other small business. One result: If you attend a craft show, you will see a much larger percentage of crafts today originating in Mexico, China, Korea, Taiwan, and other foreign countries, where labor costs and government regulation do not impede business investment and expansion, but, rather, encourage it. Even so, if you are young enough to move toward establishing a cottage industry and can handle the various roles and complications these outside factors present, financial success is possible. But beware of the pitfalls.

Once again, being the adventurous and enterprising lady that she is, Rosie plunged in head first, while we only theoretically examined the problems of the cottage industry.

Rosie's Business Adventures and Misadventures

Some years back, at the end of a financially miserable weekend, Rosie was approached by an entrepreneur who was interested in design artists and wondered if she would create bears for him. Rosie didn't take this proposal very seriously until he called again and informed her that he could provide her with some potentially big customers. He asked her to design two or three samples to present to buyers representing some nationally known chain-store outlets. Rosie agreed and provided them. The buyers liked the bears on presentation and agreed to purchase a certain number, setting the retail price at $19.95. (This was a much smaller bear than the one ordered by the Home Shopping Network.) The question then became, could she produce the required number of bears that would sell at that price and still make a profit? Fortunately, the chain stores did not expect the markup that the Home Shopping Network required. If manufactured in the United States with that large a profit built into the price, Rosie's small bears would have had to retail for at least $60. Even with a smaller profit margin, domestically made bears could not have sold for $19.95.

To make a profit at the retail price of $19.95, the entrepreneur—now Rosie's partner—went to China and, with a Chinese partner, established a small factory. Rosie went to China to supervise the initial manufacturing process. She noted that Chinese laborers, who were inexperienced in making this type of product, needed meticulous schooling, but once they learned how to do it, they produced an especially fine product—of course, at a much lower cost than American labor. She also noted that the general quality of Chinese merchandise was constantly improving. So when Rosie was satisfied with the quality of product being produced, she returned home. The total cost of producing and shipping the bears was $4. Rosie received a profit of 3½ percent. So when all was said and done, Rosie netted $7,000. It was worth her effort, since she hadn't spent any of her own money upfront. It was a one-time-only deal, but Rosie's adventure was not over.

Successful in this endeavor, Rosie, who had grown tired of doing craft shows, and her new partner established a small factory in Twain Hart, California. She incorporated, hired five people, and purchased the necessary machinery. As Rosie will readily admit, she then made her biggest mistake by not hiring at least a bookkeeper immediately. The next obstacle she faced was finding people to hire at minimum wage who had the talent to produce beautiful bears. Her partner, having invested his money, went about his own business, not realizing that Rosie had no experience running a cottage industry or mass-marketing a product. The result was that the order for bears came in and Rosie simply could not fill them. Thousands of dollars went by the wayside, Rosie went deeply in debt, and her established reputation suffered. The sales reps out in the field lost their commissions because the orders weren't filled, and the merchants had no bears to fill their shelves.

A quick attempt to put a Band-Aid on the problem led to a return to China in hopes that the orders could be filled there, but the Chinese partner had gone belly-up in another business deal, so there was no salvaging the enterprise. Since Rosie never had a backup plan, both she and her partner lost a lot of money.

The lesson that Rosie learned from all this was that, as a creative, artistic person, she should have stuck to her area of expertise and hired the accounting, marketing, and advertising personnel necessary to run a successful business. As Rosie said, "I couldn't spread myself out any thinner. I got so scattered that I ended up doing everything 'half-assed.'" When the hats don't fit, don't try to wear them!

There is a happy ending to this tale, however. Rosie did learn from her mistakes and returned to her primary area of expertise—designing bears. Her financial backer secured contracts with three major distributors throughout the United States, each requiring a differently designed bear, something Rosie could easily create. A new factory has been established in China and Rosie now has orders for 900,000 bears.

When to Retire and Preparing for It

It was these circumstances that led us to a question I mentioned at the beginning of this book: When is it time to retire? It is a question all of us in the business ask ourselves at varying stages of our careers. Some just can't keep up the pace and quit early. For others, it is a way of life and they continue until their dying breath or poor health forces their retirement.

Judy and I chose neither alternative. We felt that we had reached a stage of life when we had received all from the business that it could give and we had given all that we had to give. Our creative juices were depleted and each show became less fun and more work. It was simply time to move on to the next phase of our life. It was not a problem for us. Happily, we had anticipated this eventuality. I had retired once before, and the pension from that earlier retirement provided us with an income. We had invested some money from almost every show.

Investing that money was not always easy, and sometimes it was not as much as we would have liked, but we made a point of disciplining ourselves to do it. The choice of a good mutual fund made retirement very easy. We would not presume to offer you investment advice. But we would urge you to seek the advice of a financial planner early in your career. The day will come for most of you when you will want to walk away from the craft merry-go-round, you will want to be able to do it in style, and, most of all, you will want to do it with a sense of financial security.

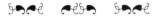

Epilogue

OW, IN WRAPPING UP THIS PACKAGE AND PRESENTING it to you, the reader, a few words should be said about general courtesy, manners, deportment, and ethics. As in any respectable profession, how you conduct yourself is continually evaluated by your fellow craftspeople, promoters, and the public. Establishing your integrity and honesty is vital to your success.

Because of the physical and emotional strain of the business, your patience and endurance are constantly pushed to the breaking point. Exhibiting at a craft show is not unlike going on stage. The curtain goes up and you have a role to play. We saw many in the business who could not separate their role as a artist from their role as a seller. As a result, they lost many customers and a lot of money.

The public doesn't know or begin to appreciate the hard work you have put into creating your work, and you cannot allow them to know. They aren't interested in listening to verbal squabbling, nor are they at a show to be pressured, bullied, or insulted. You are not there to judge them.

The customer has paid to judge you and your product. So, when the show opens, it is time for you to become your most charming, effervescent self. Treat everyone—whether they make a purchase or not—like a guest you have invited into your home. This approach pays big dividends.

The same is true of your relationship with fellow artists. You will find that, very often, you will need their help and advice, and they will request yours. As the years pass, you will see many of them over and over again. Some will become great friends, others won't. You don't want any of them as an enemy.

Yes, you are in competition, but you are not at war. Help your neighbors out when they need assistance. There will come a day when your canopy collapses or the wind causes you a lot of breakage and you'll need their help. If they are selling successfully, be happy for them. Jealousy over their success does not improve yours.

Learn from your fellow artisans and from the mistakes you will naturally make. Share those mistakes, and the way you corrected them, with others. If you become financially successful, it will probably be, in large part, because of the helpful hints and tips you received voluntarily from many people you meet along the road.

We hope that the advice we have given will not discourage you from entering the crafts business. Our intent is to enlighten and inform, so that you may approach the business in a realistic and practical manner. Beyond that, the craft world is uncharted water. It is our desire that you jump in with your eyes wide open.

For all the work, frustration, and, sometimes, tedium, Judy and I also gained a great sense of achievement and considerable financial and emotional reward from our years in the crafts business. We never lost the feeling of satisfaction that comes when you create a product and then find that strangers are willing to spend their hard-earned money to purchase it, place it in their homes, or give it to a loved one or a special friend. We felt that excitement and wonderment the day we sold our first basket and we felt it when we sold our last.

During our seventeen years in the business, we met and sold to people from all over the world. As you wrap up a purchase and hand it to the customer, or pack it for shipping, it is a gratifying feeling to know that your creation will be placed in a home in Europe or Asia or Africa or Australia. Before we retired, The Three Basketeers had a home in about twenty-five countries. That satisfaction goes beyond making money. There is a feeling of closeness to the customers and, in talking to them about the work, a sense of commonality.

Judy and I found that no matter what the customers' place of origin, at heart, they were never really very different from us. They had the same concerns, loved and cried as we did, enjoyed the same beauty, got wet in the rain, and sweated in the heat, just as we did. In few occupations can you meet so many thousands of people, of such diverse backgrounds. That also holds true of the thousands of craftspeople that we met.

For all the wear and tear and planning that the travel entails, it also took us to cities and towns and countrysides that we would never have seen otherwise. We often worked in environments that were breathtakingly beautiful, met the people who lived there, and made friends of many as we returned to the same show each year.

Our business also made it possible for Judy and I to be together on a daily basis. We had the rare parental experience of being able to spend every day and evening with our youngest son Mark, something we could not do when we raised our two older children. We were there for him on a daily basis, in ways that are impossible in the normal workaday world. We could play tennis, golf, or go for a swim when we chose. As husband and wife, we forged a working relationship unique among married couples, and it contributed greatly to the stability of our twenty-six year marriage.

We will never regret the years we gave to the business and we've never heard anyone who is successful regret theirs, either. Many of the friendships we made will last throughout our retirement years. That is why we have written this book. We want your craft adventure to be a similarly rewarding experience. Good luck! Have fun and have a great show.

About the Author

Judy and Phil Kadubec

*P*hil Kadubec was born and raised in New York City. throughout his life, he has enjoyed a varied employment history. At age eighteen, he was a Roller Derby skater until he was drafted during the Korean war. Later, he worked in Chicago as a credit investigator, an insurance underwriter, and a dancing instructor. In 1955, he graduated from the University of California at Berkeley with a major in psychology.

Following graduation, Phil took employment with the Alameda County Probation Department, in Oakland, CA, where he worked for the next twenty-two years, retiring in 1982. Deciding to leave the Bay Area, Phil, his wife Judy, and their children built a home in Blue Lake Springs, CA, where they first became interested in the craft business. Together, Phil and Judy developed the Three Basketeers, and for the next seventeen years, the couple and their son, Mark, traveled to hundreds of craft shows.

Retiring completely and selling their business in 1997, the family began a new phase of life, with Judy gardening their four acres in Smartville, CA, and working for Nevada County as a court clerk and Phil writing this book and pursuing a Masters Degree in the humanities at Cal State. Their son Mark is in the computer industry, their daughter Jenny is a homemaker in Sonora, CA, and their son Jeff is a Respiratory Therapist in the U.S. Air Force. Phil expects to teach at the junior college level and to continue writing.

Index

Books from Allworth Press

Selling Your Crafts by Susan Joy Sager (softcover, 6 × 9, 288 pages, $18.95)

Business and Legal Forms for Crafts by Tad Crawford (softcover, 8½ × 11, 176 pages, $19.95)

The Law (in Plain English) for Crafts, Fifth Edition by Leonard DuBoff (softcover, 6 × 9, 224 pages, $18.95)

Legal Guide to Visual Artists, Fourth Edition by Tad Crawford (softcover, 8½ × 11, 272 pages, $19.95)

The Business of Being an Artist, Third Edition by Daniel Grant (softcover, 6 × 9, 352 pages, $19.95)

The Fine Artist's Career Guide by Daniel Grant (softcover, 6 × 9, 224 pages, $18.95)

The Fine Artist's Guide to Marketing and Self-Promotion by Julius Vitali (softcover, 6 × 9, 288 pages, $18.95)

How to Start and Succeed as an Artist by Daniel Grant (softcover, 6 × 9, 224 pages, $18.95)

The Artist-Gallery Partnership: A Practical Guide to Consigning Art, Revised Edition by Tad Crawford and Susan Mellon (softcover, 6 × 9, 216 pages, $16.95)

Caring for Your Art: A Guide for Artists, Collectors, Galleries, and Art Institutions, Revised Edition by Jill Snyder (softcover, 6 × 9, 192 pages, $16.95)

The Artist's Complete Health and Safety Guide, Second Edition by Monona Rossol (softcover, 6 × 9, 344 pages, $19.95)

The Artist's Quest for Inspiration by Peggy Hadden (softcover, 6 × 9, 224 pages, $15.95)

Artists Communities: A Directory of Residencies in the United States That Offer Time and Space for Creativity, Second Edition by the Alliance of Artists' Communities (6¾ × 10, 240 pages, $18.95)

Please write to request our free catalog. To order by credit card, call 1-800-491-2808 or send a check or money order to Allworth Press, 10 East 23rd Street, Suite 510, New York, NY 10010. Include $5 for shipping and handling for the first book ordered and $1 for each additional book. Ten dollars plus $1 for each additional book if ordering from Canada. New York State residents must add sales tax.

To see our complete catalog on the World Wide Web, or to order online, you can find us at *www.allworth.com*.